C000090411

BACK TO THE GARDEN

BACK TO THE GARDEN

Ursula Buchan

F

FRANCES LINCOLN LIMITED
PUBLISHERS

We are stardust,

We are golden,

And we got to get ourselves,

Back to the garden.

Joni Mitchell, 'Woodstock'

Frances Lincoln Limited

4 Torriano Mews

Torriano Avenue

London NW5 2RZ

www.franceslincoln.com

Back to the Garden

Copyright © Frances Lincoln Limited 2009

Introduction, selection and editorial matter copyright © Ursula Buchan 2009

Articles copyright © Ursula Buchan 2003, 2004, 2005, 2006, 2007, 2008

Ursula Buchan has asserted her moral right to be identified as the author

of this work in accordance with the Copyright, Designs and Patents Act 1988 (UK)

First Frances Lincoln edition 2009

All rights reserved.

No part of this publication may be reproduced, stored in a retrieval system,

or transmitted, in any form, or by any means, electronic, mechanical,

photocopying, recording or otherwise without the prior written permission

of the publisher or a licence permitting restricted copying. In the United

Kingdom such licences are issued by the Copyright Licensing Agency,

Saffron House, 6-10 Kirby Street, London EC1N 8TS.

A catalogue record for this book is available from the British Library.

ISBN 978-0-7112-3017-0

Printed and bound in China

1 2 3 4 5 6 7 8 9

CONTENTS

❦ INTRODUCTION ❧

It is five years since I last gathered together a collection of my horticultural writings, which appear in newspapers and magazines. In that time, I have written several hundred more. So it seemed a good moment to see whether these still resonated with me and, if that was the case, whether they might do so with you as well. Although we gardeners may not perceive this very clearly, we deal, in our gardening lives, with the big themes: climate, nature, work, beauty, bounty, humanity, even the striving for that elusive Heaven on Earth. As a result many of those articles, which I thought might have lost their savour in the intervening period, have still a saltiness that appeals to me at least. These are the ones I have chosen and, where an article has become a little dated, but still retains some element of truth, I have included it, adding short notes of explanation where absolutely necessary. There are inevitably occasional repetitions of a favourite phrase or idea, for which I hope readers will forgive me.

Although I write for a number of print publications, the choices I have made have mainly been 'think' pieces, written under the strapline 'Borderlines' in the *Daily Telegraph* gardening section, or 'Gardens' in *The Spectator*. There are other pieces from the *Daily Telegraph*, as well. *Slightly Foxed* and *Hortus* also get a look-in, and I am very grateful to my editors Kylie O'Brien, Liz Anderson, Gail Pirkis and David Wheeler, for their support, encouragement, forbearance – and swift payment of fees.

When my last anthology appeared, someone said to me, in a tone of mild exasperation: 'There is rather a lot about you in the book, dear.' Well, yes, there is, but I am, frankly, unrepentant. When I write, I strive to connect with you, dear reader, and this is the best way of doing that. I don't affect an attitude of Olympian detachment, since that is tiresome to us both, and does not reflect my gardening experience. I am often as puzzled by my garden and gardening as you are, and I don't want to set myself apart, just because people are prepared to pay me small sums of money in exchange for printing what I write. I am intrigued, enriched, enlightened, fascinated and sometimes saddened by my garden and I imagine – or, perhaps more accurately, hope – that you are, too.

In the last five years, gardening, as we practise it in this country, has changed – enough for us to notice at least. The widespread interest in it, fuelled by 'makeover' programmes and celebrity interest, which was evident in the mid-1990s, has fallen away, as it was bound to do. It was seed sown on weedy ground, and the thistles of other interests have grown up to choke it. People have realized that you cannot make a garden in a weekend. If you could, it would be neither enjoyable nor satisfying. But, with the distant rumble of wars and crashing stock markets in our ears, more than ever gardening is a comforting and soul-enlivening occupation, which I believe is worthy of our best, finest and most enduring efforts.

Northamptonshire

1

❦ WHY GARDEN? ❦

The Spectator
4 November 2006

There are a great many good reasons for not taking up gardening. It is a subject which comes with more baggage than the England cricket team. And much of it likely to deter you. For instance, you may well, when young, have been told, in awed tones, that some grumpy old trout with a grey bun and filthy fingernails is 'a great gardener'; or there will be a family legend that your great-aunt had a brief fling with Vita Sackville-West; or you've discovered that your sister's sensitive friend does nothing but enthuse about texture, light and shade, saturated colour and developing monochromes.

As for the Latin names . . . offputting, or what? Your father has friends who potter around the garden in the freezing cold, muddy of knee from turning up the flowers of diminutive snowdrops, saying, '*Surely* it can't be just plain *plicatus*?' Honestly, it's worse than opera buffs going on about 'Cossi Fan Tooootay'. As much as the inside of your house, you fear that your garden will offer an opportunity for others to place you somewhere pretty unflattering on the Taste Scale – and, what seems particularly terrifying, you would have to be an experienced gardener to know exactly where. You worry that, if you take up gardening, it will restrict you to entertaining your friends between early October and late March, when people cannot arrive until after dark, and you can close the curtains against their desire to 'just have a look to see how your garden is getting on'. Surely the most difficult, but most frequently asked, question in the world to answer (after 'Why Jonathan Ross?', of course) is 'How is the garden?'

All that is perfectly true, but if you bother to take up gardening, you will discover a number of pluses, which may not have been immediately obvious to you before. The first is that it is almost laughably easy to grow most plants, even if you don't know much. I was forced to take up gardening seriously as a teenager (I had simply been loafing about in the garden before then). Fifteen is generally an age when you have more important things on your mind. And yet my efforts were met with the most remarkable – to me, anyway – success. My leeks, carrots and lettuces germinated, grew enormous and were harvested in due season, even though I only ever read the instructions on the back of seed packets. The borders looked absolutely fine to me once I had pulled out the bulk of the mauve-flowered opium poppies which seeded everywhere. My twin sister and I called them 'cabbages', since they had fleshy leaves and we didn't know any names, Latin or otherwise. It didn't seem to matter. Certainly, ours was a mature garden, but most things seemed to come up in the spring and die down in the autumn, much as expected. And it looked quite nice in between.

As for the roses, about which people seem to have such heebies, I sent away to a newspaper for a climbing rose called 'Compassion', because I liked the name and there was a space in front of a brick wall, and it flowered beautifully within six months of being inexpertly planted by me. Admittedly, I had picked up some rudimentary knowledge, because my lavatory reading for some years had been *Roses: Their Culture and Management*. (This appealed to me because it did exactly what it said in the title, unlike the other book in the loo, *The Wilder Shores of Love*, which for a teenager was distinctly disappointing.) Even with only a smattering of an idea of what to do, rose growing turned out to be a doddle.

Plants that you can buy in your local garden centre are meant to succeed, and they mostly do. Provided you don't actually plant something still in its plastic pot (although even that does not matter in the short term), you have a very sporting chance that it will wax strong, healthy and floriferous. If you don't believe me, why are there so many gardeners? Surely if it were really difficult, like calligraphy, say, you wouldn't meet very many people who did it, would you?

Other cheering things about gardening (and more reasons for its popularity) are that it doesn't need to be expensive, or require much space, or inevitably turn you into a glassy-eyed monomaniac. If you have a windowbox that you tend in Lambeth, you are a gardener, perfectly entitled to mutter about *Galanthus plicatus* if you want to. You are tending living things, which flower, after all. There are snobs who are gardeners, but you don't need to join their ranks. If you become a gardener, you will be agreeably surprised by how many people retain an attractive humility and self-deprecating humour, refusing to put themselves beyond the pale of civilized society – no, not even after they have started collecting African violets.

What gardening offers is the perfect, and complementary, combination of art and craft. Indeed, I cannot think of any other common pastime that so completely combines those two virtues. Moreover, it requires both physical and mental exertion, something many of us would consider the ideal for our leisure hours. Gardening often provides the closest encounters we ever have with wild creatures. It is a solace and a distraction in bad times, and a shared joy in good ones. When you are young, gardening gives you a reason to be out in the fresh air, and when you are old it is a reason to hang on grimly until the apple trees blossom once more. It can be frustrating, agonizing, boring, time-consuming and disappointing, but also uplifting, fascinating, aesthetically satisfying, mentally stimulating, sociable and even sometimes funny. To do an injury to Dorothy Frances Gurney (although I scarcely dare): you may not be nearer God's Heart in a garden than anywhere else on earth, but often it will feel like it.

'Borderlines', *Daily Telegraph*
18 February 2006

There is a lot to be said for an interest in gardening. For one thing, it helps you to come to terms with February. When I was young, February was the month in the year I disliked. The half-term was the shortest, the weather was the dreariest, there was nowhere much to visit at weekends and only rich kids went skiing. Worst of all, my mother died one February, and my childhood came to an abrupt end. Small wonder I hated it.

All that has changed now. Well, changed a lot, anyway. Gardening, along with the Six Nations Championship, has reconciled me to this shortest, but often coldest, of months. In fact, I look forward to it, since there are some intimations of spring, which you really do not get in January. Before I became a gardener, no one could convincingly explain to me what a thrill it was to see snowdrops in full flight. Snowdrops begin to flower from the end of December in this garden, but they are at their muted, chilly, most magnificent best during this month. Before I took to gardening, I could never have imagined what a sharp stab of regret I would feel each year when they start to go over. Until, that is, I catch sight of a drift of *Crocus tommasinianus*, their pale mauve chalice flowers opened wide to welcome the weak winter sun, or a squat clump of sugar-mice-pink *Cyclamen coum*, or the furled dove-grey umbrellas of *Iris reticulata*. Such sights make you forget what you have already lost and look forward to all the riches that are to come. If you have never been able to see the point of gardening, you won't know what that is like.

The jobs are not so bad, either, at least in a dry February such as this one. I know everyone in the south of England is in a lather about the lack of rainfall, and what problems there will be for water authorities and gardens later in the year; right now, however, being able to get out to paint the wooden Versailles tubs, finish the digging, prune the fruit bushes, wash the pots, chit the potatoes, sow a bit of seed in trays, even weed in those borders with the lightest soil is a pleasure to be quietly savoured. These activities make me feel I am stealing a march on spring. February is like the beginning of a party, but this time it has begun more slowly and sedately than usual, thanks to some harsh frosts and a slow-moving anti-cyclone. Nevertheless, the first guests have arrived and are standing around in isolated, self-conscious groups. There is time to get to know them properly, before the crush and noise begins. The band has not yet struck up, but there is an air of hushed expectancy. Oh yes, there is a lot to be said for February.

'Borderlines', *Daily Telegraph*
9 October 2004

As I sat at ease in the garden on an early September afternoon, the sun's warmth on my face and light breezes fretting the border grasses, grown golden in the sunlight, some words of Faust, as he contemplates a terrifying wager with Mephistopheles, rattled disconcertingly in my head.

If I should say to the moment,
Stay awhile, you are so beautiful,
Then you may clap me into irons
And I will willingly perish.

Just at that instant, I could see just how beguiling the temptation must have been, for I felt a strong reluctance to let the moment go. I wanted to freeze time, the better to appreciate it.

We have become accustomed to fine, sunny early Septembers, but this year it seemed peculiarly blessed. This was not just because the wettest August for many a long year set up such a contrast but also because the rain of that month gave the garden a fresh lease of life. Roses have had a wonderful second flowering, late-summer perennials like asters are flowering fit to bust, the lawns are lush and green, and the early autumn colours look very promising. It was the greatest pleasure to dig potatoes in the sunshine, knowing that they would dry nicely in a day before being put in sacks, to cut the wildflower 'meadow' because raking off the hay was so easy, to pick the damsons, autumn raspberries and early pears, and to remove leaves from round the winter squashes to help them ripen.

Then the wind and rain came, and I was curtly reminded that autumn was creeping on. Surely it was only the day before yesterday that the apple blossom was flowering, and the queen bumble bees flying on their first forays? How the garden has changed in those few short months!

Every year, I am newly astonished by the extraordinary, relentless dynamic of plant growth. Indeed, not so long ago, I wrote a book about it. I shan't tell you what it's called or you will think it a shameless puff, but the point of it was to show how much plants change in the course of the season, and how we can use that mutability for the benefit of our gardens. Howard Rice, my collaborator, demonstrated this vividly by photographing a number of plants at different seasons of the year. These pictures were set next to each other on the page and they surprised even us with the extent of the transformation that takes place in leaves, from spring bud to autumn fall, and the rapidity with which flowers turn to fruit. Sometimes it is hard to credit that one is looking at the same plant.

In Millennium year, I planted a celebratory avenue of *Crataegus orientalis*. I wanted a planting of garden trees that would lead the eye towards the countryside beyond the boundary, but would not jar in the rural setting. *Crataegus orientalis* is not a native hawthorn, but something fairly similar, with neat, downy grey-green leaves and white May blossom. Although this is generally a tree grown for those leaves and flowers, at this time of year I walk past them frequently for the pleasure of watching the round haws turn colour from green to cream to umber to orange to light scarlet. The differences from day to day are sufficiently marked for me to notice them. The lesson they teach is that I really have to stop wanting, vainly, to freeze the moment; I am much better employed observing it.

'Borderlines', *Daily Telegraph*
25 September 2004

My husband and I are irretrievably smug, I am sorry to say. We are smug marrieds ('Twenty-five years and never a cross word, eh, darling?'), smug country dwellers ('It would be hard to move to the city – so noisy, so much traffic') and smug professionals ('Too much work to do – haven't had a day off for *ages*'). We are also, in autumn, smug harvesters. We are smug about the fruit and vegetables we pick, smug about the honey we extract from the bee hives and, most particularly, smug about what we do with it all.

At this time of year, we are particularly keen to encourage our friends to come to stay. This is not in order to set them to work, I hasten to add (since there is something horribly beady about inviting people for the weekend to get them to pick apples for you), but, at least partly, to have them affirm the pointfulness of all this harvesting, freezing, jamming, jellying, juicing and storing. We long to have the chance to press on them damson jam, honey and home-pressed apple juice for breakfast, redcurrant or quince jelly on the lamb at lunch and every kind of permutation of berry or currant dessert for pudding. It is true that a guest will sometimes ask, through gritted teeth, whether they might possibly have the Marmite, please, but we put that down to their being too set in their ways.

Time was when all these homely activities were necessary to ensure a balanced diet, especially in the winter. Now they are simply fun, although, since I am irredeemably self-satisfied, I try to make a case for this home-made stuff tasting better than 'shop-bought', even if it sometimes gets rampant mould and has to be quickly thrown away.

It may be fun, but I am conscious that we are in a bind. We have fallen into the usual trap which catches out many gardeners, that of planting lots of fruit trees and bushes all at once, because yields in the early years are low. Then, suddenly, or so it seems, everything reaches a certain point of maturity and starts to fruit fit to bust. From then on, it is all hands to the pumps in the autumn.

This year, the problem has been particularly acute, because the lack of frost in spring and the rain in late summer ensured heavy crops of larger-than-usual fruit, while rough winds in September made the picking less than orderly. We were dashing around picking up windfalls, trying to think when we might have time to press them for juice before they rotted, while scouring the house and shed for wine boxes in which to put those picked off the trees. The self-satisfied smiles have become a little fixed.

But only a little. And only temporarily. For I know that, even if we don't pick every apple in the garden, nothing will go to waste. In October, on sunny days, we will often see a butterfly or two feeding on a windfall, while in November, we can confidently expect both the blackbirds and the fieldfares, those wonderful migratory thrush relatives from Scandinavia, to descend on the garden and polish every single last one off. By early December, there will be absolutely nothing left of that great autumn abundance; it will have been satisfactorily tidied up for another year. Which will leave us to concentrate on the aspects of the garden which are definitely not properly sorted out, especially the perennial weeds, the state of the greenhouses and the protection of tender plants. Then even we will struggle to retain our smugness. And a good thing, too, you might say.

'Borderlines', *Daily Telegraph*
11 September 2004

August has given me ample opportunity to whinge. First it was the garden flooding, now it is the flooding's aftermath. Artemisias, nepetas, phlomis, salvias and other drought-loving Mediterranean shrubs, which were planted in pockets of gritty soil amongst the paving on the terrace, have dropped leaves like ash trees in autumn or turned to soggy, disagreeable messes. Three days submerged in water has sent a number of them packing. I am a little at sea, if that is the right expression, since I have never experienced waterlogging on this scale before.

As for the *Solanaceae* family – petunias, nicotianas, tomatoes and potatoes – the effect of so much rain this month has been dramatically awful. The annuals have yellow leaves and the potatoes have been badly afflicted by potato blight, the leaves and stems of all but one variety collapsing in a heap, and having to be cut off and burned. Alone amongst the naked ridged rows, green and unbowed, is the foliage of a Hungarian-bred variety I am trialling, called 'Sarpo Axona'.

I cannot think of conditions – frequent, substantial heavy rain and high humidity – which have more favoured the spread of potato blight (*Phytophthora infestans*) but I was never even slightly tempted to spray the potato rows with mancozeb. That is because I wanted to test the much-vaunted blight resistance of 'Sarpo Axona', a row of which I had planted in the middle of my potato patch. I could honestly not have picked a better summer for such a trial. This red-skinned potato has large oval tubers, with an old-fashioned, floury texture, and has proved excellent for roasting, which allayed any anxiety that its disease resistance might have been won at the expense of taste. Its stablemate 'Sarpo Mira' will be in the Thompson and Morgan 2005 catalogue.

So, even I cannot whinge all summer long. Not only have I found a blight-resistant maincrop potato, but the day after the floods finally receded from the garden, beautiful Painted Lady butterflies arrived from the Continent to settle on rudbeckias and verbenas close to the house, warming the heart and setting the air in motion. On a more prosaic note, I have never pulled out sowthistles so easily in August, although it is true the conditions have ensured there are rather more of them than usual. This has been a remarkable year for blossom – not just fruit blossom in spring, but roses in early summer, and August-flowering hoherias and hibiscus as well. We have never known such a marvellous crop of raspberries, even if we had to do battle with the wasps to pick them, and I am hopeful of a fine harvest of good-sized apples and pears, since drought at the roots is hardly a limiting factor this year. The young small-leaved lime trees that I planted in late winter in the paddock, close to the bee hives, in the hope that one day we might enjoy lime-flower honey, were gasping for water by July, since it is impossible to irrigate so far from the house. The August rains have prompted them to make new fresh young leaves.

And, perhaps most cheering of all, a creeping little ground-cover plant called *Leptinella*, which rarely does very much but is beautifully neat in all its ways, was flooded with the rest on the terrace, yet has turned not a hair. And that despite a reputation for liking sharp drainage and full sun. So really, honestly, truly, what have I got to complain about?

'Borderlines', *Daily Telegraph*
17 July 2004

Sometimes I wish that hope did not spring eternally in the human breast. Otherwise, I would not be fooled with quite such frequency by attractive catalogue descriptions. I buy something on the strength of an intriguing or over-enthusiastic endorsement from a nursery or seed firm, and live to regret my vain optimism.

My big mistake the year before last was *Rudbeckia occidentalis* 'Green Wizard'. I had never seen it, so it was the name that sold it to me. Who could not want a rudbeckia (coneflower), a member of that most stalwart and useful of summer perennial families, which revelled in the name 'Green Wizard'? Surely this was just the long-lasting, sturdy-stemmed plant I needed to act as a foil to the scarlet and orange flowers of high summer? It was apparently 'noble' and 'ornamental', with 'nice clumps of foliage' and 'remarkable' flowers, consisting of green petal-like bracts surrounding chocolate-brown central cones. It seemed ideal: sophisticated, unusual, nicely perennial, a talking point for visitors, perhaps.

I duly sowed the seed, planted the seedlings out and waited for fifteen months for it to flower, which it did last June. Sure, the cones were chocolate-brown, but the petal-like bracts began as a dingy green and soon faded to brown with a greenish tinge. The flowers were not startling and certainly not possessed of wizardry. The stems were strong, and a 'gift to flower arrangers', although I was strangely reluctant to cut them, so subfusc was their appearance in the borders. The real problem with them, however, was that they were martyrs to snails. Within weeks of emerging, the large, green ovate leaves were tattered and holed as if they had been machine-gunned. If this is sophistication, I thought, give me 'a lovely splash of colour' any day.

This year, my mistake has been *Cosmidium* 'Brunette', which looked from the catalogue picture like a rather nice, small-flowered, yellow and mahogany-brown cosmos, which I thought might be just the ticket to accompany other hot-coloured flowers in a couple of large pots. One seed catalogue called it a hardy annual, another a half-hardy annual. The first said it would grow to 18 inches/45 centimetres, the second to 30 inches/75 centimetres, the third, 1 to 2 feet/30 to 60 centimetres. The foliage was apparently 'finely cut'. After germination, the stems grew and grew, but seemed quite unable to stay upright, which made them useless for containers. As for the foliage, 'finely cut' actually means distinctly wispy. In the end, I planted them near the front of a hot, dry border, where the main shoots trail along the ground, throwing up 9-inch/23-centimetre vertical flower stems. The flowers are undoubtedly attractive – like those of a French marigold without the military bearing – but their garden impact is limited by the thin and lax growth. To be fair, prolonged sunshine now may increase the flower power as the summer wears on. We shall see. As for the name, *Cosmidium* 'Brunette' is actually a Texan annual called *Thelesperma burridgeanum*. The thought of trying to unravel that particular mystery sent me to lie down in a darkened room.

I have no desire to bash nurseries or seedsmen. Catalogues are not sworn affidavits of fact but invitations to buy. Seed catalogues, in particular, offer so many kinds of seed that there is precious little space for expansive plant descriptions. Nor would they sell a single packet of *R. occidentalis* 'Green Wizard' seed, I suspect, if they called it 'Greenish Wizard' and added the phrase 'the perfect breakfast for snails'.

I guess I really ought to have learned by now that two of the first lessons of gardening are: 'If you don't know it, look it up in a book' and '*caveat emptor*'. I tell myself I shan't make mistakes again, but deep down I know that that, too, is a vain hope.

2

OTHER PEOPLE'S GARDENS

The Spectator
November 2006

Just as embroiderers working in the late eleventh century would not have appreciated the achievement that was the Bayeux Tapestry until they stood well back at the finish, so garden writers are usually too caught up with describing the details of individual gardens to consider the overall magnificence of 'the English garden'. It was not until I really considered the matter, when writing a book on the subject, that I began fully to understand what a tremendous collective achievement it is.

English domestic gardens (that is, those connected to a house, however big) are as much a product of society and culture as of the individual taste and inclinations of their creators, influenced, to a very high degree, by patterns of thought and fashions at the time of creation. But that, as I have discovered, is only part of the story. Not only are there fine and important gardens where trends have been either bucked or ignored, but it is plain that some pretty remarkable and original individuals have decided to give much of their life and energy to their gardens, and have influenced garden style as a result. In the case of Chatsworth, to take just one of many examples, so many generations of the family have been involved in garden making since the late seventeenth century that it is surely possible to talk of a gardening gene.

Political and economic forces have often also been important, even crucial. In recent years, garden owners have been helped by politicians, believe it or not. I know this won't appeal much to the *bien-pensants*, but the owners of large gardens have much for which to thank Margaret Thatcher and John

Major: Margaret Thatcher because her government cut tax rates, and John Major for instituting the National Lottery. We sneered at Major for his 'tax on the poor', but there is no doubt that the Heritage Lottery Fund has provided much of the fuel to power the engine of the conservation of historic gardens since 1994. There were renovations of important landscapes and gardens, such as Claremont and Westbury Court, before that time, it is true, but I very much doubt whether, for example, Croome Park in Worcestershire, 'Capability' Brown's first commission, would have been restored without the help of large tranches of Lottery money.

It may seem toe-curlingly smug to say that our gardens are the best in the world, but it may just possibly be true. Certainly a benign concatenation of factors – temperate, maritime climate and wide range of soils, in particular – means that we can grow a far greater range of plants than we are properly entitled to in such a small country; and this has meant that a number of garden styles have developed very successfully. There is, presently, a lively spirit of experimentation in the air, with adventurous garden designers given their heads by garden owners enriched by City bonuses. Forget the anxiety about the lack of skilled gardening labour these days, which seems to threaten standards. Sure, it's a problem in places, and needs to be tackled, but technological advances have undoubtedly cut the number of gardeners required. Certainly, I only very rarely came away from a garden visit wondering how on earth the owners could continue to manage.

More of a worry is creeping climate change. Garden visiting numbers have declined slightly in recent years, and this is due partly to the variety of alternative ways of spending spare time but also to a run of cold springs and scorching summers. One day this July, for example, I promised myself a trip to West Green House in Hampshire, a garden of great verve, style and originality. With the temperature at 89°F/32°C, I could not face the two-hour drive in a car without air conditioning, and so I stayed at home. What is more, garden owners are presently having to deal with a number of tree diseases, the progress of which is promoted by winter droughts and summer heat, which threaten to alter the look and balance of large gardens, in particular. Even where these diseases are not a problem, garden creators have to rethink established plantings, especially those using thirsty plants, which conditions now make unrealistic. However, I have absolutely no doubt that they will rise to the challenge.

Frankly, I defy anyone not to have the breath squeezed out of them when they consider the number, range, complexity, floriferousness and serene beauty of those English gardens open to the public. Garden visiting remains one of the most agreeable and innocent ways of spending leisure hours – one which we certainly shouldn't take as much for granted as we do. Individual gardens may rise and fall but, collectively, they remain one of the enduring glories of England.

The Spectator
July 2004

I do not have much objection to television garden makeover programmes, strangely enough. It is certainly odd for anyone to think that it is possible, let alone desirable, to make a garden in a weekend and expect it to stay made, but I see the point of encouraging a youngish generation, with no background of gardening, to have a go, and find out for themselves the satisfactions inherent in the process.

There is, however, one way in which most television gardening does thoughtful gardeners no favour. Proper, grown-up, contemporary garden design is obscured by the emphasis on DIY decking, solar-powered water 'features' and glass bead gravel. Only at the Chelsea Flower Show time does it emerge briefly, like the lazy fin of a carp breaking the surface of a deep pool. The first Modern Gardens Day,* held on the last Saturday in June, was intended to show that much else is possible – with thought, creativity and often, although not always crucially, with oodles of dosh.

Because of the jejune nature of television gardening, gardeners can be forgiven for thinking that nothing very momentous has happened to public and private gardening in the last twenty years. But that is far from the case. For a start, garden design is now an accepted and respected profession, with its own society and journal. Perhaps because of this, a number of strong twentieth-century traditions have been losing their grip. The Jekyll planting tradition has given ground, as its high-maintenance impracticality becomes ever more glaring and we finally become bored with harking back to that Edwardian golden afternoon. The 'new perennial planting' is well established in the mainstream, thanks in particular to Keith Wiley, Piet Oudolf and Noel Kingsbury. We have also become much less insular. Foreign designers, such as Alain Provost and Alain Cousseran (Thames Barrier Park), Piet Oudolf (Scampston Hall and Pensthorpe) and Wirtz *père et fils* (Alnwick Castle and the Jubilee tube station at Canary Wharf), are praised and fêted.

Strict minimalism, formalism with a contemporary twist to it and adventurous naturalism all seem acceptable these days. Although pre-war Modernism never took the hold in this country that it did on the Continent (perhaps because concrete looks so drab in the rain), it does not mean we do not appreciate asymmetry or the abstract, and we certainly respond favourably to, for example, Charles Jencks' sinuous landforms at Portrack and Edinburgh's Gallery of Modern Art.

English Heritage, which, together with the Association of Garden Trusts, sponsored the Modern Gardens Day, deserves credit for its Contemporary Heritage Gardens initiative at Osborne House, Portland Castle, Richmond Castle, Eltham Palace, Witley Court and Lincoln Bishop's Palace. English Heritage has employed the darlings of contemporary garden design, such as Christopher Bradley-Hole, Mark Anthony Walker and Rupert Golby. This suggests an understanding that large, important gardens have always grown organically, in the sense of piecemeal and gradually, and that there is no uncomfortable paradox in an Elizabethan house having an eighteenth-century park and a twenty-first-century walled garden, provided that all is coherent, congruous and of excellent quality. This view has plainly also been taken by the Legards at Scampston Hall in north Yorkshire as well as the Chambers at Kiftsgate Court in Gloucestershire, where the third generation of owners has added their own spin, in this case a new minimalist garden with pool where once there was a tennis court.

The gardens open on Modern Gardens Day were quite eclectic, the only common feature being that they had all been made, or partly made, in the last few years. They ranged from the Arts-and-Crafts Movement-influenced Bryan's Ground in Herefordshire, to Great Fosters in Surrey, where Kim Wilkie (who won the competition to redesign the courtyard at the V&A) has shown that it is possible to ameliorate a very modern problem, namely traffic noise from the M25, by creating a landform turf amphitheatre and massive planted earth bunds. One of the more refreshing aspects of contemporary garden designers is that they don't pretend that things are not as they are.

Gardens with clever colour schemes, such as Helen Dillon's in Dublin and Marylyn Abbott's at West Green House in Hampshire, were well to the fore. Modern planting, even when it is not influenced by Continental ideas, is much less a matter of painting by numbers, as it was in Jekyll's day, and more about intermingling and repetition. The effect requires more skill to achieve but, as I discovered on Modern Gardens Day at Broughton Grange near Banbury, it can work well. The Walled Garden created by Tom Stuart-Smith has a strong and clean structure of paths, allées and pool, but wonderfully exuberant naturalistic planting on the topmost level. No chance of achieving all that in a weekend, I am afraid.

There has been only one Modern Gardens Day since, more's the pity.

The Spectator
July 2008

If your ears go back, like a frightened horse, at the word 'conceptualism', when applied to modern art, you may not be very pleased to know that this is a hot topic in landscape design at the moment. Before you gallop off round the paddock, however, I should point out that we could all be beneficiaries, if the result is brighter, more interesting public (and private) spaces. After all, there cannot be much to be said for the rigid geometry, concrete street furniture and off-the-peg greenery that have been the norm for decades. At a symposium on the subject, organized by the Society of Garden Designers and held at Tate Britain last week, the mood was enthusiastic, optimistic, even excited. There was a recognition that conceptualism encourages a refreshing inventiveness in landscape and garden design.

According to Tim Richardson, whose recent book *Avant Gardeners* (Thames and Hudson) contains a consideration of the work of fifty design partnerships worldwide who work at least part of their time in this way, conceptualist garden design is the harnessing of an idea, or related ideas, as the starting point for work characterized by the use of colour, artificial materials (such as recycled glass, for example) and a visual commentary on a site's history, culture or ecology. It often blurs the line between art and landscape. It can be witty, thought provoking, beautiful even, although, it must be said, it is sometimes downright daft.

Conceptualism is only another way of expressing the very human desire to make sense, in an innovative and engaging way, of our world – which, let's face it, is what drives many people to become gardeners in the first place. Conceptualist landscapes and gardens can have a function, but it is not central as it would be to Modernism; and, though they can be flower-rich, they are demonstrably not in the tradition of British decorative horticulture. Many have a sustainable, ecological theme, not surprisingly, but the best are those which pay homage to their surroundings rather than wrench the spectator's attention round to ponderous fears about global threats.

Conceptualist designers are great ones for show gardens, as witness their fondness for garden shows such as Cornerstone in California, Jardins de Métis in Canada, Chaumont in France and Hampton Court Flower Show (where the Royal Horticultural Society for the last three years has encouraged the participation of half a dozen conceptualist designers, with impressive results). Of course, creating a show garden is a very different matter from designing something that can carry its intellectual load over the long term, and these garden shows tend to encourage 'one-liner' designs. That is an ever-present danger with conceptualism, but at least these shows give an opportunity for designers to stretch their imaginations, and for potential clients to see their work.

The problem can come with the real thing, when conceptualist layouts are often the target for brain-out-of-gear criticism – as was meted out, for example, to the Diana, Princess of Wales memorial fountain in Hyde Park, designed by Gustafson Porter. (Not only does the fountain say a great deal about both the appeal and the danger of the late Princess, but it is a beautiful structure in itself and will be enhanced further when the trees around it have had time to grow up to make a glade.)

What is encouraging about the conceptualists working at the moment is the heterogeneity of their vision. They are hard to pigeonhole. Claude Cormier plumped for glossy red concrete tree trunks at the Palais de Congrès convention centre in Montreal, while Ron Lutsko has made botanically and ecologically nuanced 'Sustainability Gardens' in Redding, California. The English installation artist Julia Barton uses plants in her sculptures, while the German Herbert Dreiseitl, a designer whom Richardson calls a 'maker of liquid narratives', is preoccupied with water in all its possibilities. And a number of them, like the Swedish Monika Gora, and the Americans Martha

Schwartz and Topher Delaney (she of the monster shopping bag planters), have a lively sense of humour.

But, stay, have we not been here before? What is the early eighteenth-century English landscape garden, at its most refined, other than the expression in land form of an idea, in that case the longing to inhabit a classical Arcadia, complete with temples and pavilions, and Elysian (sheep-grazed) Fields?

So, although we private gardeners will probably always remain attached to our nineteenth-century style of decorative horticulture, which warms our hearts and breaks our backs, there really is nothing to be frightened of in this conceptualist stuff. And, especially if we live in cities and have gardens limited in size, we should at least allow the ideas of Schwartz, Lutsko, Michael Van Valkenburgh, Paul Cooper *et al* to seep into our consciousness, and accept that there might just be intriguing possibilities for us as well.

'Borderlines', *Daily Telegraph*
5 November 2005

Recently I visited a garden in Kent, which is open to the public, called Goodnestone Park. You may know it. If not, I recommend a visit, since it is very fine. It is set out around a Palladian-style house, and generations of the same family have left their mark on it. There is a seventeenth-century, beautifully kept, walled garden with a view of the Norman church in the distance, an eighteenth-century landscaped park, a twentieth-century woodland, containing amongst many treasures the tallest and most marvellous *Cornus controversa* 'Variegata' I have ever seen, a Millennium parterre, and a beautiful new gravel garden made out of an old tennis court, by Graham Gough. The garden receives two stars from *The Good Gardens Guide*, only one of three gardens honoured in Kent, so you can assume, rightly, that it is top bananas.

I reflected on the way home in the train on the reasons I had enjoyed my visit so much, and it occurred to me that there had been an added ingredient, beyond its setting, design and plantsmanship. That ingredient was quiet, the only sound being that of birdsong. We all subscribe to the view that gardens are, or should be, places of peace and tranquillity, but the truth is that far too many public gardens these days are dogged by traffic noise. Aeroplanes are a curse for gardens situated near major airports (I know at first hand, because I have worked at Kew), but almost everywhere the low rumble or drone of constant road traffic nags away at one's concentration and contemplation. We private gardeners, who suffer traffic noise, try hard to become inured to it, but our gardens are not commercial garden operations, which attract visitors partly by the unspoken promise of that elusive, precious quality – quiet.

Obtrusive, discordant noise has become a much worse problem for public gardens in recent years, since so many towns and villages have been bypassed, for those bypasses often run very close to old country estates with gardens open to the public. There are plenty of advantages to bypasses, but they are not an unqualified good.

Near to where I live is the incomparable Elizabethan survival Lyveden New Bield, a place of transcendent atmosphere and beauty, set on the top of a hill in a seemingly quite remote pocket of rural Northamptonshire. If you ignore the size of the surrounding fields, you could almost imagine yourself back in the time of the ill-fated recusant Catholic Sir Thomas Tresham, whose extraordinary unfinished summer pavilion and moated garden so haunts the landscape. Yet, on race days at the nearby Rockingham Motor Speedway, tranquil Lyveden cannot escape the throaty whine of highly tuned cars and bikes. In such a setting, I find the noise as inescapable and unpleasant as toothache.

Kent is a county more affected than most by trunk roads but, somehow, the countryside around Goodnestone Park has remained rural, criss-crossed mainly by empty winding lanes. I am told by George Plumptre, whose family own

Goodnestone, that the only noise they hear is the faint one of trains when the wind is in the west. How lucky they are! There are plenty of reasons for visiting Goodnestone, when it is open between late March and early October, but not the least of them is its atmosphere of rural calm. Long may it remain so.

'Borderlines', *Daily Telegraph*
7 May 2005

All right. I'll own up to it, though most unwillingly. I am one of those odd people who posts leaflets through people's doors at election time. Besides being slightly weird, doing this can be unnerving, since most houses now have letterboxes with internal brushes, so I have to poke the flimsy leaflets through with my whole hand and risk it being savaged by a bad-tempered dog.

I do this for a variety of reasons, not all of them very high-minded. Sure, I think the democratic process very important and am convinced that apathy withers the spirit, but I am also too idle and good-natured to refuse requests for help from the relentlessly cheerful and enthusiastic local candidate. And, shamingly, I find that passing in and out of every front garden on the way to the letterbox gives me a splendid and legitimate excuse for looking hard at what gardeners are up to in my locality and, by extrapolation, elsewhere.

This year, I have carried out my election campaign in a glow of bright golden yellow. The daffodils have been everywhere and it is pleasant to see how popular miniature narcissi, especially garden cultivars closely related to species, have become in gardens, in pots and in borders alike. 'Jetfire', 'Jack Snipe' and 'Peeping Tom' are everywhere.

The biggest thrill of this leaflet trudge, however, has been a close-up view of a magnificent, mature specimen of the great white cherry, *Prunus* 'Taihaku', which, for some reason, I had never before even glimpsed when passing in the car. This is an ornamental cherry, which makes a great umbrella of large, pure-white single flowers. I am also more and more convinced now of the virtues of *Amelanchier canadensis* as a small garden tree, with its white star flowers backed by bronzey-green young leaves. As for the ornamental crab apple trees, they are a joy, their red buds so fugitive but promising so much.

This election, called for early May, has been a campaign of blossom and daffodils, with red tulips coming to the fore late on. The 2002 election, on the other hand, was a month later, so I swooned my way round the houses in a fragrant cloud of early roses – *R.* 'Maigold', *R. banksiae* var 'Lutea' and *R.* 'Nevada' – as well as the oh-so-scented, single-flowered *Philadelphus coronarius*. There seemed something piquantly ironic about seeing so much philadelphus in flower, since the name means 'brotherly love', an impulse which was in very short supply at that election. And at this one, come to that.

There is more to be learned from this walkabout. It is possible to see the effects of gardening programmes and articles, with water 'features', decking, coloured gravels and groups of containers on display here and there. But I also see how sturdily resistant some gardeners remain to voguish fashion. They grow what they want to grow, very often, not what some bloke in a T-shirt on television tells them to grow. In many gardens this spring, there are still wallflowers and forget-me-nots with tulips poking through, to be followed shortly, I have no doubt, by carpets of busy Lizzies and petunias. This twice-yearly bedding out is something gardeners have been doing for 150 years. Politicians may come and go, but gardening habits which were formed at the time of Gladstone and Disraeli survive to this day. I find that strangely cheering.

The Spectator
March 2003

The property bubble may be finally popping, but for people like me who like staying put, the recent hike in house prices, in the cities especially, has been peculiarly painful. I, who live in a less popular locality, have watched, with consternation, as people younger than me have blithely bought second houses on the strength of the ascending values of their first homes. For someone of settled habits, it is unsettling. Being prone to pompous pronouncements about the way weekend houses bleed the life out of small local communities, especially rural ones, I find it hard that no one appears to take a blind bit of notice.

However, in this atmosphere of sour, self-righteous envy, I have one cause to gloat. And I make no apology for doing so. In my experience, few weekenders manage to make a really satisfying garden – either for themselves or any onlooker. They may be able to lock the door on Sunday night, secure in the knowledge that the electricity is switched off and the fridge door open, so that all will be as it was in five days' time, but no one can freeze the growth of plants in the garden. (Many of us with just the one home don't have much time in the week for gardening, I grant, but there is always the chance, in the summer at least, of nipping out for an hour's vital weeding or sowing after supper, or before leaving for work in the morning.)

I base my infuriating assurance about this on the fact that I was once a (most reluctant) weekender myself. In my early twenties, my siblings and I owned a small house in a Wiltshire village. It was our home, most of our belongings were there, but we were attempting to make our way in London and elsewhere, so it was perforce left empty between Sunday and Friday nights.

I knew all about the dynamic of plant growth. How the spinach would bolt in summer heat like a frightened rabbit, while *Clematis montana* strangled the 'Albertine' rose on the wall and a cloud of thistledown greeted my arrival after any length of absence. Worse still, there were some favourite, precious and expensive plants, such as *Paeonia mlokosewitchii*, which flower for no more than ten days, that I often missed completely. One year, when I was temporarily working abroad, my brother kindly sent me photographs of the crab apple trees in blossom.

Plants ordered by post would invariably fetch up at the front door on Monday morning, and be half shrivelled five days later. And I was never at home when anyone who might have something for the garden called round. The first intimation that the long-ordered manure had finally arrived was when a steaming heap in the front garden was caught in the headlights as we arrived late on Friday night. Since the house fronted the village street, I can only too well imagine how unpopular we were with our neighbours. Even if we could have afforded or got hold of part-time gardening help, it is unlikely that anyone would have felt very committed to a garden in which they never saw the owners. And, without personal direction from me, any gardener, however experienced, would have had every chance to muck things up.

There was one compensation, it is true. Touring the garden in the dark with a torch on arrival was always exciting, often revealing as it did newly unfurled flowers in the beam, although just as often only slugs. Those pleasures are open to me now, when I return from a weekend or holiday elsewhere, but more rarely and less intensely.

If you are in this position, what should you do? The stratagem adopted by sensible weekenders (of which I was not one) must be to design and plant a garden that stays relatively still. That means plenty of 'hard landscaping': paths, walls, terraces and no lawn. Greenhouses and conservatories are quite out of the question, although sowing seeds in a windowsill propagator is not. Well-behaved evergreen shrubs and trees, as well as repeat-flowering roses, have to take a larger part than higher-maintenance perennial plantings, while deciduous plants need to have more than one season of interest (say, fruits and autumn colour as well as flowers) if they are to earn their place. It is all possible, but needs a great deal of thinking about to prevent it being deadly dull.

After five years of often pointless toil, we sold the house and garden, just at a time when the latter was beginning to look like something. I had tried out several design and planting ideas quite successfully, but the maintenance was always too exigent for the garden really to please me. I remember it with affection, but not much regret. If you are planning to buy a second home with a garden, I hope that the same thing won't happen to you. Do I really mean that?

The Spectator
July 2007

This spring, I paid one of my periodic visits to the Eden Project in Cornwall. There was, as always, a great deal to see and admire. But, as always, I found the didactic, and sometimes decidedly naïve, content of the information boards too relentless for enjoyment or edification. Didacticism is the business of an educational trust, of course, but, at times, the hectoring tone risked undermining the cause. For example, the Eden Project is pitching for £50 million of Lottery money for a new building called the Edge, where the public can learn about the impact and challenges of climate change. What could be more worthy or more important? The guidebook reads: 'As a wise person once said, "If you're not on the edge, you're taking up too much space."' As my husband, also a wise person, said: 'Nonsense written in a good cause is still nonsense.'

The Spectator
October 2004

Gardeners are not often happy with their lot. Even if they have bought a house specifically for the garden that surrounds it, nothing will be quite right. The soil will be too light or too heavy, too stony or too chalky, too moisture-retentive or free-draining, too acid or too alkaline. If there is an aspect, it will be too windy; if it is sheltered, there will be no view. As for the climate, if you live in

London, the season starts too early but August is a write-off; in Devon, there is not enough frost to suit the rhubarb; in Essex there is not nearly enough rain, while in Argyll there is far too much. Whenever two or three gardeners are gathered together, there is likely to be an organized, harmonized whinge.

I am no different from anyone else. After all, my garden is on heavy clay and situated in north-east Northamptonshire. Enough said. The advantage of whingeing, of course (even if it is wearisome to the listener), is that any successes are gained against the odds, and are all the more impressive as a result. Just occasionally, however, even I am forced to shut up complaining, when faced with the real difficulties other gardeners encounter.

This August I spent a few days in Sutherland and, while I was there, I visited most of the gardens that are open to visitors in that most thinly populated of all counties, as well as next-door Caithness. It was a salutary lesson. For in Sutherland, at a more northerly latitude than Moscow, the growing season is at least four weeks shorter than that in the south of England, with the possibility of frosts in every month except July. The minimum winter temperature is minus 41–50°F/5–10°C and rainfall 30–40 inches/90cm–1.01 metres. There are ferocious winds to contend with, as well as sea mists (haars) which roll in from the sea regularly and rapidly, sending temperatures tumbling.

So how does anyone make a good garden there? In times gone by, Scots perfected the building of walled gardens, setting them on south-facing slopes if they could, and with open-slatted garden doors at the bottom which would let the frost drain away. Walls cannot keep out fogs, of course, but they can create favourable microclimates. At the House of Tongue, at Dunbeath Castle and at Langwell, for example, tall walls enclose the gardens, making it possible to grow a surprisingly wide range of plants, especially fruit, vegetables, hardy shrubs and perennials, as well as providing back walls for glasshouses, where even figs and apricots may ripen.

Within these walls, borders, often hedge-backed and laid out with care, are as colourful and full of variety in July and August as they are a month earlier in the south of England, with sweet peas, annuals, massed ranks of herbaceous perennials and roses. The raspberries and cabbages were the finest I had ever seen.

Not all the gardens are large ones, created by Scottish landowners and timed to be at their best in the grouse-shooting season, of course. Mrs Elizabeth Woollcombe, an accomplished plantswoman, has lived at West Drummuie, half a mile from the Dornoch Firth near Golspie, for thirty-four years and she has no walls, except those of the house. Her solution has been to shelter the garden from the salt-laden east winds with *Griselinia littoralis*, escallonias, olearias and hebes, many of them brought back as seed from New Zealand. Hers is an intimate, informal, woodlandy garden on a south-facing slope, where every plant is known and cherished. Mrs Woollcombe will be ninety in November, but is as lively, curious and interested as can be, and spends most of each day in the garden.

She conducted me round the garden, where we stopped at many a rarity and, with the true gardener's generosity, gave me seeds and plants. She excitedly showed me a callistemon (Australian bottle brush) grown from seed sown twenty-five years ago, which was flowering for the first time. On our way back to the house, she pointed to some adjacent land, which she said she was hoping she might be able to take in and make into a garden for children to enjoy. Attitude, not latitude, is what matters, it seems. I take my hat off to all the hardy Scottish gardeners, who do their best with what they are given. And don't complain about it.

3

ART AND BOOKS IN THE GARDEN

'Borderlines', *Daily Telegraph*
11 June 2005

I have always taken masses of photographs of my garden. In the past, I have used a compact camera with the facility to stamp the date on the print, so that I could see exactly when they were taken, so vital to anyone making a garden. But the business of getting the prints developed and putting them in a book (well, more often scribbling 'GARDEN 2005' on the envelope and 'filing' them in a drawer) has meant that I have never used them as much as I might. Which is why I found myself recently trudging grumpily to a camera shop to buy a digital camera. Grumpily, because I am, by nature (though not by intent), a technophobe and I was worried that I would have to grind through a handbook the size of the Paris telephone directory, written by a heartless geek. I feared the thing would sit in its box unused because I would never be able to understand the instructions.

But I had reckoned without the reassuring nature of people who work in camera shops. In my experience, they are usually male and often have an adventurous taste in both ties and moustaches, but they are patient, knowledgeable and enthusiastic, and careful not to make it too obvious that they think I am a daffy female who should not be let loose with anything more technical than a hairdryer. After twenty minutes, I felt sufficiently confident to buy a camera, with five megapixels, no less. I found loading the software easy and, though the modest-sized handbook was rather more of a challenge, a fortuitous holiday gave me the chance to work through it systematically. And, to my enormous surprise, I discovered that the camera took terrific pictures, with an excellent sharpness and depth of field, without my doing anything more exhausting or complicated than pressing the button and waiting for it to stop whirring. Captioning and filing on the computer took a little more application, but I mastered that in the end as well. And I soon discovered that I could enlarge or enhance the image if I wanted.

I have spent this spring snapping away in my garden every few days, and am beginning to see clearly fault lines in the planting which I could never properly put my finger on before. These pictures already constitute a valuable reference archive. But the real revelation was the Chelsea Flower Show. As anyone who goes on the Members' Days knows, juggling a camera with notebook, pencil, handouts, catalogues and spectacles in a crowd of people is not an entirely delightful experience. This year, however, I simply pointed the camera at any plant I wished to record, making sure that I had the label also in view, and pressed the shutter button. The notebook was still vital when I wanted to ask questions of exhibitors, but much of the time it stayed closed. Having spent two days at the show, I then whiled away two happy evenings downloading and captioning the pictures, frequently astonished by how well the images had been captured. All this you probably know perfectly well, but it was a revelation to me. When next someone asks me what is my favourite tool for use in the garden, they may be bemused to be told that it is a Canon Ixus 500.

Technology has moved on very fast since I wrote this piece and I now have a Nikon D40 SLR, with appropriate lenses, which is far better. But I shall not quickly forget the excitement I felt when I first appreciated the possibilities a digital camera held out to the gardener.

Daily Telegraph
Chelsea Flower Show Supplement
May 2008

It is generally agreed that botanical art is presently enjoying a renaissance, as the opening of the new £3 million Shirley Sherwood Gallery of Botanical Art in Kew Gardens last month bears witness. Amongst the artists that Dr Sherwood admires, and whose work she collects, is Bryan Poole, an ebullient, erstwhile rugby-playing, documentary maker who trained as a botanical artist at Kew. He makes copperplate etchings, using the painstaking and meticulous *intaglio* ('in the cut') technique, which was developed in Europe in the sixteenth century.

Bryan Poole shows his hand-coloured etchings each year at the Chelsea Flower Show, and this year he has two pictures on display, which are likely to cause something of a sensation. Each portrays the flower of a tropical heliconia species – just visible inside the enormous, gaudy, orange-red bracts – being visited by the gorgeous purple-throated carib humming-bird (*Eulampsis jugularis*). In one, the male bird is visiting *Heliconia caribaea*, in the other the female visits *H. bihai*. These pictures tell an amazing tale of co-evolution or what the scientists call 'ecological causation of sexual dimorphism and co-adaptation'.

Dr John Kress, a botanist at the Smithsonian National Museum of Natural History in Washington, together with an ornithologist colleague, Ethan Temeles, has, for some years, been studying the relationship between *Eulampsis jugularis* and two species of heliconia. They have discovered that the female birds have long curving beaks, which exactly fit the lengths of the flower throats of *H. bihai*, from which they take nectar and which they pollinate, while the males have shorter, straight beaks, which fit the flowers of *H. caribaea*.

Dr Kress met Bryan Poole when Shirley Sherwood was showing his pictures, as part of an exhibition she was curating, in Denver, Colorado, so last year Dr Kress asked him to make copperplate etchings of this extraordinary interaction between heliconia and hummingbird. Bryan travelled with him to Dominica, and tramped into the forest to look at these heliconias and hummingbirds, and to make preliminary scale drawings and watercolour sketches. On his return, he visited the Natural History Museum, where he was able to observe Gould's stuffed hummingbirds. This was, he says ruefully, a relief, since the Dominican montane forest is exceedingly damp and, moreover, these hummingbirds beat their wings eighty times a second and are 'like little blurs'.

The testing process of making copperplate etchings requires impressive stamina, artistry and dedication. Mistakes cannot be unmade. First Bryan makes a linear drawing with an etching needle on to a copper plate through a resin 'resist', which is impervious to acid. Then he immerses the plate in ferric chloride acid, which bites into the metal wherever the resist has been removed by the etching needle. After that, he uses complex and time-consuming aquatint and 'spit bite' aquatint techniques to give a tonal effect, rather like a wash drawing. (These are techniques that were used by Redouté and Goya, amongst others.) Final highlights are achieved by burnishing back into the surface of the plate in order to expose the linear structure of the image. This results in a highly textured image of great depth and surprising vitality.

After that, he uses seven different inks to hand-colour the plate, using a scrim or *poupée* dipped in ink. The plate is then steel faced, to protect the fine details from being worn away too quickly in the printing process. Finally, he puts the plate on to the bed of a nineteenth-century Rochat *intaglio* press, lays moistened acid-free paper on to it and then turns a wheel (a task that requires all his physical strength) to press down on the paper to make the print. Finally, when dry, the print is hand-finished, using watercolours. Remarkable to me is the fact that the copper plate is etched back to front: Bryan must have an exact idea of the finished composition before he begins. The prints are limited to a hundred; after that, even a steel-faced plate will progressively lose its sharpness.

What makes these heliconia and hummingbird pictures so wonderful is that, despite their artful design and rich colours, they are scientifically accurate. The differences in flower structure of the two heliconias are as clear to see as those in the shape and length of beak. The white background forces the eye to look through the two-dimensional image, so that it acquires tremendous depth – something promoted by the design of the leaves, stems and flowers.

It was in July 1858 that Charles Darwin and Alfred Wallace revealed their theories on natural selection to the Linnean Society of London. On Darwin's visit to the Galapagos Islands, he had studied ground finch species, which had evolved with diverse beaks, depending on the food types available; these came to be known as 'Darwin's finches'. Exactly 150 years later, what people are calling 'Darwin's hummingbirds' will be there for us all to see on Eastern Avenue.

The Spectator
December 2007

As I spend much of my life in a flower bed, bottom up, I rarely consciously make the connection between the flowers that I grow in my garden and their more elevated associations, in particular their role in Christian art. Only when I visit art galleries or churches am I forcibly reminded that garden and wild flowers appear again and again in paintings, as well as featuring prominently in the plastic and applied arts.

This is hardly surprising, since flowers were both comprehensible and universal symbols in pre-literate times, and have remained enduring signs of Man's appreciation of the beauty and variety of God's creation. This was brought home to me the other week in Kraków in southern Poland, when I went to reacquaint myself with the Art Nouveau stained glass and murals of Stanisław Wyspiański.

Wyspiański (1869–1907) is not a name to conjure with in this country, more's the pity, except amongst his compatriots living here, of course. Where he is known, it is usually as the author of *The Wedding*, written in 1901, which earned him a reputation as the first modern Polish playwright. But Wyspiański, who was born and spent most of his short, illness-dogged life in Kraków, was much more than a prolific playwright: he was poet, city planner, furniture designer, illustrator, sculptor, printmaker and painter. He attained the Polish ideal of a deeply religious patriot, at a time when Kraków was part of Galicia, a province of Austria-Hungary. He was a prominent member of the Young Poland movement. This year, the centenary of his death, has seen a clutch of celebratory events in Kraków.

My Polish being still rudimentary, I couldn't really join in with those, but I sought him out in the churches of central Kraków. He began his church work by helping to design the stained glass in the west end of the great St Mary's Church, which dominates the Market Square. He also restored the stained glass in the nearby Dominican Church after the disastrous 1850 fire which swept through the middle of the city. However, his greatest achievements are the wall paintings (polychromes) and stained glass to be found in the Franciscan Church, close to where Pope John Paul II lived when he was Karol Wojtyła, Archbishop of Kraków.

The west end window is entirely taken up by an enormous and overwhelmingly powerful stained-glass image of God the Creator (*Let it Be*). On the side walls, however, are murals depicting some of His humblest creations, notably dandelions, sunflowers and blue chicory, while cheerful pansies are painted entwined in a geometric grid, as if growing through a trellis. In the transept, there are bright orange and yellow nasturtiums, and beautiful pink and white roses. As a counterpoint to God the Creator, at the east end of the church, above the high altar, are six stained-glass windows. The two central ones encompass relatively small figures of the Blessed Salomea (an aristocrat who founded the church in the thirteenth century) dressed in the habit of the Poor Clare she became, and St Francis of Assisi. These figures are surrounded by summer flowers, especially graceful Madonna lilies, beautifully wrought. The other windows show the four elements, depicted by characteristically Art Nouveau flowers and sinuous abstract shapes. Most fascinating and beautiful for me were the images of tall mauve and purple Siberian irises, and dumpier yellow and white water lilies, set in swirling waters. Even on a gloomy day in November, they glowed.

What touches me, as a gardener, about Wyspiański is that he took such care over the minute botanical exactitude of flowers in his murals and stained glass, while still managing to use them decoratively. This is true also of the work he carried out in the interior of the house owned by the Medical Society of Kraków (ul. Radziwiłłowska 4). Here, as well as a stained-glass window of Apollo, he designed metalwork balusters for the central staircase, in the shape of stylized horse-chestnut leaves and flowers, a design which he echoed in a painted ceiling frieze above.

A piece of the balustrading is on show in the Wyspiański Museum (ul. Szczepańska 11), where there are also the studies he made for the church murals and stained glass. When I was in Kraków, winter was tightening its grip on the city, snow was lying and temperatures were well below zero but, thanks to this remarkable man and the flowers he depicted, in the museum and in the Franciscan Church at least, it was eternal summer.

Slightly Foxed
February 2004

Once upon a time, or until about 1960 that is, there existed a genre of horticultural literature called, colloquially, 'the chatty gardening book'. In fact, the phrase did these books less than justice, for they were generally interesting, amusing, literary works written by educated, cultured people for the edification of an equally educated gardening readership. I collect as many as I can find in second-hand bookshops for, even if the spelling of plant names in them is sometimes archaic, they are still a pleasure to read in the winter, especially in bed.

The genre is scarcely alive these days. For the last twenty years, the highly illustrated book, which is large in format, expensive to produce, full of dreamy, 'inspirational' colour photographs and often with a truncated and colourless text, has been the order of the day. The quality of garden photography is so high, the images so winning, that, in the words of the American writer Charles Elliott, 'it's pretty difficult for mere prose to match the grandeur of a photograph, in full glowing colour, of a perennial border in high summer, say – especially if the photographer thought to use a sky filter'. There are still, however, one or two publishers (and it is a pleasure to single out for praise Frances Lincoln and John Murray in particular) prepared to publish, for the quality of the writing alone, small, modest-looking hardback books containing nothing more by way of illustration than a few line drawings, and sometimes not even that. I have been a beneficiary of this enlightened outlook and so plainly has Charles Elliott, whose *The Potting Shed Papers*, subtitled 'On Gardens, Gardeners and Garden History', was published by Frances Lincoln in 2002 at the reasonable price of £14.99.

Strictly speaking, this is a reprint, being a collection of essays first published in that most up-market of American gardening magazines, *Horticulture*. They are really home thoughts from abroad, for Charles Elliott lives in London and makes a garden in Monmouthshire. Indeed his earlier books are entitled *The Transplanted Gardener* and *A Gap in the Hedge: Dispatches from the Extraordinary World of British Gardening*, which give you some idea of his angle. Like the late Henry Mitchell, Allen Lacey, Eric Grissell, Michael Pollan and Eleanor Perényi, he is a member of a much underrated – this side of the Atlantic – group of highly intelligent gardening writers with the gift of making their musings both readable and intriguing. But Elliott seems the most valuable of them all to us Anglocentrics, because he lives over here. Britain and the United States are separated by a common horticulture just as much as a common language. We often use the same tools and the same expressions – with the exception of the word 'sod', of course – yet we are nearly always divided by differences of climate, soil, plant varieties and, most especially, bugs (that is, insect pests).

So it is a delight to come across an American in sympathy with us, yet sufficiently detached to laugh gently at our foibles and point up our idiosyncrasies. Elliott's writing is wry, and dry as a vodka martini. He does not pretend to be a gardening expert, although he seems pretty knowledgeable to me. But, as he says, 'Fortunately . . . there . . . seems a place for those of us content merely to potter around the subject, peering from the outskirts, happy to explore its more curious, amusing and unexpected aspects.' He certainly has found plenty of those.

In *The Potting Shed Papers*, he writes on a great variety of subjects: on plants, such as the peripatetic peony, on people – anyone from Joseph Rock to Geoff Hamilton – and on what he calls 'husbandry', which includes botanical names, how to keep records and the description of a notable garden designers' spat entitled 'Design and its Discontents'. He seems never happier than when he is sitting engrossed in the Royal Horticultural Society's Lindley Library in London, ferreting out arcane historical facts: for example, that Père Delavay, an obscure French missionary in China in the nineteenth century, sent back to France 200,000 dried plant specimens, representing at least 1,500 species new to science; that the coastal redwood (*Sequoia sempervirens*) is named after a half-Cherokee scholar who invented a written language for his people; or that our humble (and threatened) house sparrow was introduced into the United States to eat the snow-white linden moth caterpillar and is now the commonest bird to be found there.

There is one notable difference between this book and earlier ones written by English authors like E.A. Bowles or Reginald Farrer, Eleanor Rohde or A.T. Johnson, H.E. Bates or Beverly Nichols. Those books, although laboriously put together by printers without the aid of computers, almost never contained a typographical error. There are a disturbing number in this volume, usually words mysteriously missing. For a man who was once senior editor for the New York publishing house Alfred A. Knopf, that must be peculiarly painful.

He knows his Marcel Proust, Gerard Manley Hopkins and Henry Longfellow, which is consoling for any reader who thinks they might be wasting their time on 'just a gardening book'. They certainly would not be. I find this is an obvious choice for bedtime reading, since it is small enough to be held easily in one hand. Two chapters a night are enough, though, for facts are scattered as thickly on its pages as groundsel seed in my borders. This book is certainly elegantly written, but it is also quite dense. It is like a rich pudding, which is best when savoured slowly and reflectively.

4

THE CRAFT OF THE GARDEN

'Borderlines', *Daily Telegraph*
6 January 2007

At this time of year, I begin to feel a distinct twinge of guilt. My decision to give up winter digging some years ago still has the power to unsettle me. 'In the old days' I would hope to have finished the digging in the vegetable garden by now, and would have the hands, like blistered paintwork, and aching back to prove it.

I was brought up to dig. When I trained at Kew, weeks in the winter were spent double-digging the Order Beds, where different botanical plant families were grown, every time one of them was to be replanted. It was a torture, made worse by the fact I was not naturally a tidy worker, yet double-digging was considered a touchstone of horticultural expertise. In those days, no self-respecting practical manual of gardening was without its mystifying diagrams, with lines marked out, arrows showing where the next spit of soil should be put, the position of the heaped wheelbarrow and so on.

I knew that you only needed to do this when making new borders or vegetable beds, or when compaction was a real problem, but single-digging (that is, digging over the soil to the depth of the spade, incorporating organic matter) really was, and mainly still is, an annual event in vegetable gardens and allotments everywhere. In gardens with heavy soils, the solid spit-shaped blocks of clay should be leaning against each other by Christmas, waiting for the frost to 'break them down' into that blessed state, 'the friable tilth', by spring. That is, if we get enough frost to do it these days.

However, when we moved to a garden with soil with which one could easily have made house bricks, I rebelled. It wasn't a conscious decision, really, for my training could not suddenly be unlearned or disregarded. That would have seemed heretical. It was just a recognition that I had more pressing things to do in the garden which precluded me from doing anything in the late autumn except skim off, with a sharpened spade, the annual weeds which had grown through the autumn, and then spread a 6-inch/15-centimetre layer of rotted manure on to the vegetable beds. Four months later, the manure would have almost disappeared. The mighty earthworm, coupled with winter rain, had seen to that, aerating the upper level of the soil in the process, and providing nutrients in liquid form to plants, the only way in which they can take it up. What was still lying on the surface could just be lightly forked in. No blistered palms there.

I am not claiming that digging can never be beneficial. Incorporating both air and organic matter into soil can be a good thing, in compacted soils in particular. It is just that, if you do a cost/benefit analysis, digging usually doesn't add up. Most of us live extremely sedentary working lives and as a result a sudden burst of intense physical activity such as digging is more likely to do us harm than the garden good. My undug vegetable garden flourishes, at least partly because digging upsets the soil eco-system, disturbing the growth of mycorrhizal fungi, which increase the capacity of plant roots to take up water. Digging also throws up annual weed seeds, which germinate before I can sow my seeds in spring. Come to think of it, why on earth should I feel any guilt at all?

'Borderlines', *Daily Telegraph*
15 January 2005

Those who work outside in winter are quickest to notice when the days begin to lengthen. Years ago, when I was a green under-gardener, Mr Willis, my superior, told me that he reckoned the days started perceptibly to draw out on 12 January – and he was right. (He was right about most things. He told me a lot of other gems, about gardens, about the natural world and about rural life before the war, as we pruned the glasshouse peach trees or swept leaves together.)

After that, every year that I was employed as a gardener, I would look up on 12 January at a pink, freezing-clear afternoon sky and mark the fact that, for the first time in six weeks or so, I would be going home in the light. Now that I no longer have to be outside in the dark days of early January, I have lost that small but intimate connection with the turning of the earth.

'As the days lengthen, the cold strengthens' was another piece of wisdom from Mr Willis, and even recent climatic trends would not have changed his mind entirely. This is the moment when the flowers of my favourite early snowdrop – an enormous *Galanthus elwesii* hybrid called 'Maidwell L' – show their clean, cold whiteness against grey-green, fleshy leaves. This is a sight as warming to my heart as the fieriest of autumn leaves or the sweetest of summer roses. Most years, however, a short freezing snap will cause the galanthus leaves to flop, as if exhausted by the cold, reviving only when the temperatures rise once more.

I have lost something, I know. If you are paid to be outside working, the trudging nature of gardening in January can be dreary, but it makes the rewards of unfurling aconites, irises and hellebores so much the richer than if you simply view them from the warmth of your sitting-room.

Professional gardeners are there to catch the fugitive, delicious scents of *Lonicera fragrantissima*, *Hamamelis mollis* or *Chimonanthus praecox* as they go about their work. January is surprisingly busy for the employed gardener, unless the weather is really wintry: planting bare-root trees, sowing early vegetables under glass, digging, sorting through the potting shed, cleaning and servicing the machinery and tools, making seed lists, washing pots, tending the compost heaps, putting down mole traps, pruning apple and pear trees, laying new paths, renovating borders . . . so the list goes on.

Though I have left their ranks, I still find it in me to envy the many hundreds of gardeners working in what was once called 'private service', as well as heritage gardens, botanic gardens and public parks. True, they are badly paid, not always well managed and often isolated, but they have a distinct *esprit* that comes from hard-won expertise in a complex, worthwhile profession.

So, when you look out of the window this morning and decide that you won't go out today, as the weather is not very nice and there is no task really pressing, spare a thought for those gardeners who began their weekend duty hours ago, caring for plants in glasshouses which need daily care, even in winter.

And, especially, spare a thought for the 'single-handed' gardeners, whose working life is spent on their own and who do not even have the consolation of someone to talk to, as Mr Willis talked to me, years ago.

'Borderlines', *Daily Telegraph*
12 March 2005

I recently received a press release about a lawn-mower maintenance kit. Couched in relentlessly upbeat language, it outlined the advantages of my servicing and tuning my own mower. For less than a tenner, I could avoid the necessity of sending it away to be serviced each winter. I would not only save myself from expensive repair bills, it claimed, but also enjoy (enjoy?) mowing my lawn while knowing that I was caring for the environment. It all made perfect sense.

Nevertheless, a cold hand clutched my heart, as it does whenever my thoughts turn to the subject of machinery: the years fall away and I am back in the lecture hall at Kew, battling to understand the difference between two-stroke and four-stroke engines and make head or tail of a splash-feed lubrication system or the correct way to calibrate a sprayer.

I suppose I must have passed the machinery exam in the end, since I received my diploma, but surely only by sheer force of will; I felt no sympathy or connection with the subject at all. That's not to say I didn't enjoy driving machinery – the dumper truck was my particular joy, since you could get up a fair speed in the furthest, least visited purlieus of the gardens – but what happened beneath the bonnet or casing never seemed to have much to do with me. Then or now.

I am a fool, of course. Servicing costs money. The basic price for the rotary mower is £50; that's before you consider parts or delivery. This maintenance kit would apparently give me a spark plug and air filter, fuel stabilizer (whatever that is) and fresh oil. Yet I feel a strange reluctance.

The odd thing is, I love small tools and gadgets, and am certainly prepared to hammer vine eyes into the wall, or sharpen the secateur blades where necessary; it's the internal combustion engine that really gives me the heebie-jeebies. I'm sorry to say that I feel a certain resentment towards my husband, just because he has a feeling for these things. He has a cerebral and sedentary occupation, which prevents him from taking a very active part in weeding the garden, of course, yet he is quite prepared on a Saturday afternoon to dismantle the cutter deck on the ride-on mower if the blades have struck a big stone, or replace the drive belt when it comes adrift. He will then very patiently show me how to do these things, to prevent him being called away from the study next time it happens. Ha! I don't even know which spanner to use.

And yet it was I, not he, who fidgeted, sighed and slept their way through that long, dull term of machinery lectures. After the passing of many years, however, I can honestly say that my brain has been rubbed clean of mechanical knowledge. Induction stroke, compression stroke, power stroke, exhaust stroke ... what did it all mean? No, please don't tell me – I would rather help keep the lawn-mower people in business.

The Spectator
May 2008

So a little light housework or gardening cuts your stress levels, does it? Well, I never. I long ago developed a 'ten-minute gardening' scheme for stress-busting, and I could not recommend it more highly. I keep a bucket near to hand, containing hand fork, kneeling pad and Atlas Nitrile gardening gloves. (These are like surgeon's gloves, and ideal for weeding, since they are as sensitive as rubber gloves, but breathable, and easier to get on and off.) Then, whenever I have a spare ten minutes – waiting for the rice to cook, or a telephone call, or a programme to start – I go outside to weed. In a week you can do an hour's weeding this way without realizing it, and that will mitigate the stress inherent in watching the rain spoil a free Sunday afternoon, which had been pregnant with horticultural possibilities. It's cheering how long the satisfaction afterglow lasts. There is a further refinement: 'ten-second gardening'. If you keep knife and string in the bucket, you can tie in the clematis by the back door as you wait for your husband to find his car keys. Try it.

'Borderlines', *Daily Telegraph*
3 July 2004

I wonder if gardeners ever quite get used to the variability of each season. Certainly I do not, or not enough to be blasé about it at least. This year has been typically atypical. In the part of Northamptonshire where I live, a hot, dry summer last year was followed by a remarkably dry autumn, and then a mild and only averagely wet winter, no late frosts but a very wet late April and early May. The blossom this spring was heartbreakingly beautiful and profuse, the grass grew thick and lush, and the sun shone, so everything looked its best. I revelled in the brilliance of it all.

Then, in mid-May, the rain stopped, as if a tap had been shut off. The sun shone hotly, the wind blew witheringly and the early June garden, though floriferous, began to show signs of stress. The small amounts of rain evaporated. Plants which would 'normally' last three weeks, such as peonies, went past their best in a matter of days. That lax, loose abundance of spring was well and truly over, and before its time. As deadheading and cutting back became suddenly urgent, unlooked-for gaps appeared in borders. Out from cold frames and the standing ground I brought the big, beefy half-hardy annuals, like *Nicotiana sylvestris*, *N.* 'Lime Green', sunflowers, heliotropes, petunias and cosmos, as well as the dahlias, with batches of April-sown zinnias for the front of borders. These plants looked a little startled by their sudden transplantation but soon settled down under a beneficent regime of liquid feeding and some welcome rain in late June. Thank goodness for the half-hardy annual and perennial.

This season has taught the perils of complacency. It is too easy to think, lazily, that the sheer number of plants which naturally flower in early summer, allied to benign weather, will always conspire to make it a magical season. Mmmm. Experience has taught me that this is exactly the moment when I must school myself to plan for future summers. That may sound counter-intuitive, even perverse. But, surely, now is the time to nail those unsatisfactory associations, those dreary combinations, those awkward gaps? Only when deficiencies are hitting you in the eye are you really spurred to do something about them.

Even for idlers like me, it is not difficult. It requires no more than gathering together a camera, notepad, some bamboo stakes, plastic labels with holes at one end and a ball of garden string. A compact 35mm camera loaded with good-quality Fuji colour film is about the most useful garden tool I possess,* because I can set it to mark the date on the prints. Over a number of years, I have built up an archive of pictures showing the garden, or parts of it, at particular moments of the year. (Anyone with a digital camera can do the same thing even more easily, no doubt.) When I shuffle these pictures, patterns emerge and plans form. Then it is time to march into the borders to poke bamboo canes into the ground near target plants, attaching a label to the cane with the relevant information ('move to front of yellow border in autumn'; 'split and spread out in September'; 'fill this gap after geraniums over'). This is also the moment when I make notes of which half-hardy annuals to sow next spring, especially those with vigour and presence, using this season's seed catalogues still hanging about the house. As for plants and bulbs, midsummer is just the moment when mail-order nurseries send out their catalogues to potential customers. All I need now is some typically seasonal rain to chase me indoors.

* *Or was, before I acquired my first digital camera in 2005.*

'Borderlines', *Daily Telegraph*
13 August 2005

Two things saddened me last week. The first was a report saying that there is such a shortage now of skilled gardeners that some heritage gardens may have to be grassed over. The reason cited was poor pay. Young horticulturally minded people would, we are told, rather be better-paid, more glamorous and highly regarded garden designers instead. The other event was the death of Harry Dodson, the 'Victorian Kitchen Gardener', who shot to fame in the 1980s as the co-presenter of four series of BBC television programmes, which detailed the complex work of gardeners in the heyday of 'private service'. The two events have a bearing on each other.

When Harry Dodson became a 'garden boy' in 1934, there was an established apprentice structure: garden boy, improver journeyman, journeyman, foreman, head gardener. Gardeners moved frequently to 'better' themselves and, crucially, there were masses of young men doing the same thing. Men worked hard to become eligible to be senior gardeners, so that they would get a house with the job, and could then marry. A combination of new social circumstances after the war and harsh economic realities in the 1960s and '70s put paid to this system. Outside the very large estates, if gardeners remained at all, they had usually to work single-handed. The prospect of isolation as well as poor pay began to put young people off.

I started my gardening life in 1974 in a country house garden, working under a head gardener, who liked things done 'in the old way', so I got a feeling for how things had been for Harry Dodson and his contemporaries. The mutually respectful, dignified relationship between employer and employed that he and I knew could scarcely survive into an age suspicious of deference, but the rigorous practical education, delivered with gruff kindness, has stood me in very good stead. It is the little refinements developed over many years and passed on from head gardener to apprentice that make for satisfaction (and sometimes an enjoyable, if reprehensible, sense of superiority). Refinements which were learned when quality mattered most of all, and labour was so cheap that there could be time for everything: how to tie plants to stakes securely, how to water seed trays, how to put together a glass barn cloche, how to trap earwigs, how to sharpen my knife properly, how to thin grapes.

I have, shamefacedly, to admit that, after five years' horticultural training, I took up journalism, but that was because I was just married, and wanted to have children. If I had been a man, I like to think I would have answered an advertisement for a gardener in an historic garden or large country house estate. I would have been hard up, and possibly sometimes lonely, but I would have absolutely loved it nevertheless. I cannot always hide my envy when I go to interview professional gardeners.

Gardeners may never make any money, but they are rightly proud of their considerable skills and, in my experience, usually at peace with themselves. Which is why it seems so sad that young people don't want to go into the profession any more. And what troubles me is, if they don't, who on earth is going to lay out and maintain all those beautiful gardens designed by young garden designers?

'Borderlines', *Daily Telegraph*
14 August 2004

These days, we all agree with each other that young people should be encouraged to cultivate their gardens. Television programmes and magazines dish out great dollops of advice to beginners on how to tame their newly acquired neglected wilderness and lay it out as an earthly paradise. I am all for it, of course. Why should I not be, since I began gardening seriously as a teenager, and am mightily glad I had the chance to start so early?

I have also just spent twenty years assiduously, although not always fruitfully, trying to interest my own children in gardening, in the hope that something might rub off, for when they have gardens of their own. At times they have been compliant and enthusiastic, at others bordering on the bolshy, but they see the point – if not now, exactly, then at some point in the future. I have already promised to help them with plants and advice, and even perhaps labour, when they finally get their first gardens.

But gardening media attention, like youth itself, is wasted on the young. They, frankly, have other things to be getting on with. There is no getting away from the fact that the excitement of growing plants and laying out a garden (except in as much as it can be made into an awesome party venue) will leave a great many of them absolutely stone cold.

Although it goes against the Zeitgeist even to breathe this out loud, I am afraid to say that the best years of a gardener's life are the middle ones, after the whirl of child-rearing is over but before the knees begin badly to creak. From that time in your life, in fact, when you cease to be really active participants in your children's affairs, and become cheering spectators instead. When free time is no longer spent on freezing touchlines, in school halls or puzzling over someone's homework, and when gardening must be a snatched ten minutes before work, or a hurried Sunday evening before the light fails. Suddenly, or so it seems, an afternoon will stretch out delightfully, full of possibilities and with no family commitments to dent or circumscribe it. That is when the real fun begins.

Successful gardening requires a number of characteristics that are not conspicuously connected with youth: patience, the capacity to slow down one's heartbeat to the steady pace of a task and, most of all, a trust and belief in the permanent. It is hard to be a committed gardener when you could be absolutely anywhere in six months' time. No one feels much like working for someone else's eventual benefit.

It takes experience to know that gardening is one of life's great consolations. By the time most people get to forty, they have stacked up their share of disappointments and blighted hopes, yet a sunny Saturday morning in the garden, when all concentration must be centred on pricking out tomatoes, or pruning the raspberry canes, or wrestling with dividing iris rhizomes, can be balm to a wounded soul. And, if it is glimpses of the eternal you seek, do they not reside in a breath of lily scent, a butterfly settled on a verbena flower, a tree dripping with pears?

Once beyond a certain age, people discover – even if they are reluctant to bruit the fact abroad – that gardening is the most fun you can have when wearing an old mac, floppy hat and wellington boots. That even the grind of a day's weeding can be deeply, if sometimes obscurely, satisfying. It is terminally uncool to say so, I know. But I just have.

The Spectator
August 2006

I was standing in one of those dress-shop changing rooms that has mirrors on three walls, when a thought struck me like a thunderbolt. I had been trying on some very pretty, thin-strapped summer dresses, to wear to a party, to which I was much looking forward, and where I wished to look my best. I suddenly realized that there was not the slightest chance that I could carry off wearing any one of those pretty dresses since, somewhere along the way, I had acquired beefy upper arms. I might still just about be able to squeeze into a size 10 (only half of the readers of *The Spectator* will realize what a proud, if smug, boast that is) but, whatever I wore, would have to have sleeves. I was hit by another, equally unpleasant, thought: that it was all the fault of the gardening I did. Years and years of pushing loaded wheelbarrows over uneven ground, lifting 80-litre bags of compost, mowing, strimming, carrying heavy watering cans and pulling recalcitrant hoses had given me muscles of which Charles Atlas himself would have been proud.

Why had no one ever told me that this would happen? When I became an employed gardener, at the age of twenty-one, half the world was horrified at the supposed waste of my (indifferent) degree, while the other half was lyrical in their praise of gardening as an occupation promoting mental stimulation, physical well-being and spiritual refreshment. I chose to listen to the second half, of course, but, of those, not one single person ever said to me that, although I would enjoy it, I would one day have to reckon with lorry-driver's arms.

Nor did they mention broken and cracked fingernails, a twingey back and, in later life, arthritis. I have been fortunate so far in avoiding the bad back, and assiduously do warm-up exercises on winter mornings to fend one off, but I shan't escape that fate in the end, nor yet the stiffening of joints.

And what of the sunburn in summer? My hands and arms, up to about the position of my biceps, are mahogany brown, and I have a V-shaped spread of tan on my neck. The rest is snow-white, since taking off one's T-shirt exposes one to scratches from roses, not to mention comment from the neighbours. Not for me an all-over honey-gold sun-bed tan. If ever I do dare to wear anything décolleté at parties, that sunburned V looks ridiculous, especially in photographs. I quite see Miss Bingley's point, when she sneered at Miss Elizabeth Bennet for having grown 'so coarse and brown', as a result of travelling in the summertime. Coarse, brown and weatherbeaten, that is the lot of the gardener.

The conspiracy of silence about the disadvantages of a life of gardening is complete. I am breaking cover, and bravely owning up to my physical imperfections, because women need to know the risks, especially now that they comprise a substantial proportion of the professional gardener workforce.

The reasons for the gender shift are mainly economic. Gardening, especially in the private sector and in nurseries, is a poorly paid occupation, considering the skills required and the hours worked; men with a family and mortgage in prospect (tied houses being, mainly, a thing of the past) cannot easily contemplate it. However, their wives can and do, very often taking to it as a second career. Whenever I go to meet a garden owner, these days, there is more than an even chance that I will also meet a female head gardener.

Undoubtedly, the trend has accelerated in the last thirty years, a time when women have invaded a great many former masculine preserves. For the truth is that, if modern equipment and machinery are sensibly used, there is very little a woman cannot do. I have even known one or two prepared to climb into trees with chainsaw in hand. Recognition of this can be found in the 'Come into Horticulture' booklet produced by the Royal Horticultural Society and Horticultural Trades Association. Indeed, at a time when there is a severe 'skills shortage in the industry', in the jargon, women have gone some way to saving the day, as they have as priests in the Church of England. The booklet shows lots of happy, smiling, feminine faces. But would there be so many if these girls knew that they risked becoming bruisers?

My advice to any parent whose girl shows ambitions to become a gardener is: don't let your daughter do a National Diploma in Amenity Horticulture, Mrs Worthington. Or not if you want her to feel confident and soignée at smart summer parties, that is.

'Borderlines', *Daily Telegraph*
24 September 2005

Even now, nearly four weeks on, I can't quite believe that I was actually at Trent Bridge on the Sunday of the Fourth Ashes Test. I still carry the ticket in my diary to remind me of that Day of Days. A year ago, when I bought the tickets, I imagined that, although England had improved greatly, the Aussies would, by then, be two or three up in the series, and cruising. But it would still be fascinating to see three remarkable Australian bowlers, Warne, Lee and McGrath, bowling in the flesh. By the time the day dawned, however, I (along with the rest of the country) was in a lather of anticipation and excitement, and I had become rather ashamed of my earlier pessimism.

The tension was tremendous* and the batsmen tried to relieve their stress by frequently dabbing and tapping at the pitch with their bats, patting down real and imaginary bumps and divots in an activity known, rather sweetly, as 'gardening'. Which amuses me, for the groundsman's job is very different from the gardener's.

Groundsmen go to such great lengths to mow almost all the grass off the wicket that, from the stands, what is left looks like a coconut mat. It is not so very complicated on paper, although I imagine very difficult to do well in practice. Cricket balls bounce and grip on thickly interwoven grass roots, not on grass blades. Those grasses are a mix of Chewings fescue, creeping red fescue, browntop (common bent) and modern dwarf perennial ryegrass. These fine-bladed varieties can withstand mowing down to less than 1 millimetre. The trueness of bounce and pace of the pitch, however, come from persistent rolling, using progressively heavier and heavier rollers as the spring wears on, so that the soil under the wicket is compacted hard to a depth of 4–5 inches/10–12 centimetres. These huge rollers are used between innings to keep the wicket firm. The pace of the ball, and how much it 'turns', are affected by how long water has been withheld before the match, and therefore how dry the surface is, but that is all part of the groundsman's art.

The only time you could say that groundsmen and gardeners coincide in their grass care is in the autumn, when they scarify, spike, top-dress and fertilize, just as we gardeners do (or ought to), to get rid of dead thatch, to relieve the compaction until the following year and to feed the grass roots.

Unlike groundsmen, we rarely use cylinder mowers these days, preferring the convenience of rotary mowers, despite the rougher, longer cut. Compaction is caused on our garden lawns not by mower rollers but by children playing, or too much foot traffic. We need to scarify, spike and top-dress to cultivate healthy grasses and minimize moss growth. To be truthful, I don't particularly enjoy these autumn lawn tasks, but I much admire those greenkeepers who do.

And I especially admire the cricket groundsmen in Nottingham who do almost all the 'gardening' that is necessary on the wicket at Trent Bridge.

Cricket enthusiasts will know, of course, that on that day, England had to make only 129 runs in their second innings to win the match. They wobbled horribly, and it was left to two bowlers, Ashley Giles and Matthew Hoggard, to see England safely home at the end of a very long, exciting day. In the end, England beat Australia and took the Ashes from them, for the first time in eighteen years.

The Spectator
September 2003

'The trouble with you garden writers,' said Judith Blacklock, editor of *The Flower Arranger Magazine*, not unkindly, when I met her at the Chelsea Flower Show, 'is that you don't write sense about flower arranging.' I blushed but did not demur. To be truthful, in the nineteen years that I have been writing for *The Spectator*, I have never written a word about flower arranging, sensible or otherwise. How to cultivate a rugby pitch, yes; how to distinguish between different species of bumble bees, sure; how to arrange flowers, no. Until that moment, I had always maintained, smugly, that I was more interested in living flowers than slowly dying ones. For me, arranging flowers at home consisted of plonking garden flowers in a pretty jug. Yes, I was indeed a plonker. Suddenly, however, this seemed just an excuse for idleness and timidity. Judith invited me to attend a one-day course at her school in Knightsbridge and, since she 'specializes in beginners', I accepted gratefully.

It was a pleasant, highly practical day, where we (female) students were introduced to both classical and contemporary 'floral design'. We were reminded of the four principal elements of design – colour, texture, form and space, and of the importance of scale, good proportions and 'rhythm'. We learned about 'conditioning', that is, how to prepare flowers and foliage, and the importance of mixing flower shapes. We were taught how to create 'handtieds' – impossible until you get the hang, then dead easy – which *are* intended to be just plonked in a large vase. I took home three handsome arrangements of my own making. It had been a lot of fun.

Classic flower design, as taught there at least, seems exuberant, relaxed, even 'naturalistic', with a generous mixture of garden and florists' flowers used in a loose symmetry. In a way, it is a microcosm of traditional border design, although until then it had not dawned on me (goodness knows why not) that flower arrangements are simply temporary versions of the plant associations with which I daily grapple.

One reason I was keen to learn was our daughter's looming twenty-first birthday party, for which I was both too mean and too intimidated to contemplate engaging a professional florist to provide arrangements suitable for a number of long trestle tables. Armed, therefore, with Emily's choice of colours (pink, white, blue and grey), Judith's advice on the number of flowers that would be necessary for each table arrangement and my knowledge of what the garden might yield, I ordered what seemed huge quantities of flowers and foliage.

Tucked away on an industrial estate, I found a florists' supplies' warehouse, filled with racks of gold spray paint, ribbons and other 'mechanics'. Here I bought bricks of foam 'oasis', rectilinear plastic trays to hold it, sharp knives to cut it, thin tape to secure it to the trays and bendy wire for stiffening foliage.

The day before the party, a number of enormous, shallow cardboard boxes were delivered, full of pink and white roses, blue cornflowers and larkspur, glaucous-leaved *Eucalyptus parvifolia*, variegated pittosporum and other foliage. My twin sister, Laura, and I set to work at a table in the shade of a large umbrella in the garden, to separate the various floral elements into buckets of water. The lazy Susan from the dining-room was commandeered as a turntable.

Laura is also something of a 'just put it in a pretty vase' merchant, but with impressive humility she listened while I passed on something of my new-found knowledge: soak oasis for only fifty seconds or else it will crumble; try to achieve an oval outline, using foliage before flower; keep the arrangement low so that people can see across the table. We worked on a template arrangement together, which we would copy.

However, as I was i/c marquee, generator, wine deliveries, mobile lavatory (we plumped for the 'Tennyson' rather than the more modest 'Brontë', you will want to know) and exploding balloons, I was often called away from the task and Laura did most of the work. By clever selection of flowers and foliage from the garden – rosemary, ceanothus and adult ivy foliage, 'Loddon Blue' lavender, white achillea, heuchera, grass flowers and much more – to ring the changes, she had achieved sixteen arrangements by the end of a long summer's day. These were placed on the floor of a darkened room until they were needed. All were subtly different from each other, yet unified by a strong colour theme. The effect was charming and, it must be said, looked highly professional without being stagey: far less the result of my instruction, I know, than Laura's innate artistic sense.

After the party, we disposed the arrangements about the house. They were keen reminders of a really enjoyable bash but, within a few days, were looking quite sorry. With a vase, the shortest-lived flowers can be removed without much effect on the others, but these arrangements were all or nothing. If I removed the dying flowers, I was left with expanses of pock-marked oasis. In the end, it was a relief to throw them out. Formal flower arrangements, I now see, are essential for the decoration of public buildings, like churches, as well as for special domestic occasions but for every day, I still prefer a pretty jug.

The Spectator
November 2007

The party is almost over. One of the best autumns for many years is coming to an end, the leaves finally seared off the trees by stormy weather. Even people who do not generally notice these things have been moved to comment on the richness and variety of the colours of trees and shrubs, in woodland, parks and gardens and along bypass embankments. Not only have the reliable beeches, field maples, bird cherries and birches been magnificent, but many trees which do not colour vividly every year, such as poplar, willow and hornbeam, have also turned well. My fruit trees, in particular apricot and mulberry, but also pears and apples, have taken on deep yellow hues.

This flare-up has come about through a happy concatenation of circumstances: heavy rainfall in summer meant that there was still some moisture in the ground, so the leaves did not drop prematurely, while sunny days in September and October boosted sugars in the leaves, and a lack of harsh frosts prevented a precipitate fall.

The weather has often been balmy and sunny, so we gardeners have felt a strong impulsion to be outside. 'Hurry in autumn, tarry in spring' is the old saying, but many people must wonder what precisely they should be hurrying out of doors to do. Attentive readers over the years will know that I rarely offer practical advice, since that sort of thing may be found elsewhere; nevertheless, I feel the urge to tell you how I spend time in the garden in autumn, just in case you are in a quandary about it.

I do not cut down the stems of every herbaceous perennial in autumn, as gardeners were wont to do years ago, preferring to leave those which have seed heads for scavenging birds, and to give myself something attractive to look at on sunny, frosty days in winter. But that does not mean that I think borders need no attention at all: far from it. Late autumn seems to me the best moment of all to deal, without chemicals, with perennial weeds, which are, let us face it, the bane of every gardener's life. By these I mean couch grass, perennial nettle, creeping buttercup and, most particularly, bindweed. So I remove those perennials which won't provide much sustenance or shelter for wildlife in winter, or which badly get in my way, and then set about digging up the roots of weeds that surround them.

I am a connoisseur of roots. I can instantly tell nettle from buttercup, field bindweed from ground elder, couch from Yorkshire fog. Anyone can do it with a little practice, and the knowledge is priceless. My garden *bête noire* is bindweed, whose oval leaves and searching, spiralling shoots are so deleterious to the look of a border in late summer. At this time of year, however, I have a grudging respect for those fat, white, bendy roots as they emerge at the end of my fork tines, still attached to thread-fine lianes of dried stem, which led me to them in the first place. These roots are not for the compost heap. Even small pieces can grow again, so they must be burned, if you are allowed to light a bonfire or, if not, secreted in the dustbin. Those who don't care to do that can lay them out on paving for a week to dry up completely and then put them in the compost bin.

Each garden has its own particular weed flora, depending on the acidity and constitution of the soil, as well as the locality. I have bindweed, perennial nettle, creeping buttercup, couch grass and even cow parsnip (hogweed) because I have a country garden, as well as a number of unusual weeds like wood avens. On the other hand, I need not battle with ground elder, for some reason, and, not having an acid soil, I am saved from both sheep's and common sorrel.

You may say that digging the soil disrupts valuable mycorrhizal activity, as well as bringing annual weed seeds to the surface to germinate, and you would be right on both counts. But, on balance, it is more important to banish perennial weeds and, at the same time, aerate the soil, which gets stamped down in the course of a season. You may also say that this is damn dull work, and I would not demur, although the vision of a cleaner (though never clean, of course) garden next season has the power to keep me going. For what was the iPod invented, if not to sweeten dull but necessary hours in the garden? In any event, the days are short now, so no task need be done for very long, and the frosts will come, d.v., and we can turn our thoughts towards Christmas. A successful, exhilarating party is almost over, and soon we can subside into armchairs, tired but happy.

'Borderlines', *Daily Telegraph*
4 December 2004

December is not a good month for gardeners. The days are short, the weather chancy, the tasks humdrum and even, sometimes, wearisome. The colour has bleached out of the borders, the roses are pale shadows of their summer glory and delicate plants are battered and bowed. The frosty sunny mornings, when seed heads are picked out in rime, are rarer in reality than the illustrated gardening books would have us believe. Much more common is a cold, relentless drizzle weeping from a leaden sky. There is quite a lot to do (especially after an autumn like this when weeds like sowthistles have grown so magnificently) but the conditions do not often suit either border or gardener. Moreover, when there is a rare bright Saturday morning, you find it dissipated writing Christmas cards or queuing grumpily to park in the shopping centre. We gardeners have to tread water, really, until mid-January, when the days start to lengthen and the snowdrops and aconites appear.

But there is one particular perk of this time of year, for those of us whose thoughts are never very far away from the garden – even, or perhaps especially, when sitting in a parking queue. And that is the pile of gardening gift catalogues, which have fallen through the letter box this year as thickly as autumn leaves.

Who can resist the siren call of all those intriguing little horticultural sundries which might just make all the difference to gardening success next year? I am not referring to the irritating croaking china frogs, the epoxy resin simpering deer or the bamboo wind chimes with which these catalogues are often rather cluttered. I can pass all these over without a sigh of regret. No, it is all those thingamygigs, such as the outside tap frost protector, the telescopic weed knife for removing weeds from paving, the topiary shears, the bamboo cloches for protecting dahlias and the handsome wooden twine dispenser, for which my soul yearns. I am even sorely tempted by the tool which makes plant pots out of old newspapers, even though, in my experience, plastic pots breed in the shed as freely as coat hangers in the wardrobe.

Every year, at this time, I am tempted to send off an order for a number of these 'indispensable' (they are always indispensable, in cataloguese) tools and sundries. Sometimes I even get as far as computing the p. and p. and writing out the cheque. Then I hesitate, ruminate and finally tear it up. Self-knowledge, fitful and flickering as it is, kicks in. I know, deep down, that there is no gadget on earth, however alluring its description and ingenious its manufacture, which can really make a substantial difference to the success of my gardening. In small ways, these things may improve some aspect of the garden, but such improvement will be perceptible only to me, I suspect, and only because I am looking out for it. More often, they get one outing, and then are put on a shelf in the shed and forgotten. The successful gardener is one who has the courage, tenacity, strength and time to dig and divide, plant and prune, weed and rake, observe and learn, plan and execute. No amount of daisy grubbers or terracotta plant labels can make much difference to that. What these thingamygigs do, however, is to make gardening just a little bit more fun. And fun is what we gardeners sometimes need – especially in December.

The Spectator
December 2004

In our garden, there is a two-seater, brick-built privy. It hasn't been used for forty years or so, but its presence in the garden still has a direct influence on my gardening. Not only does the present paved path follow the direction of the original rough concrete one which led from house to privy but, more importantly, the soil in the borders close by is freer draining and more friable than that to be found anywhere else in the garden. The effect of the annual cleaning-out of the privy – I am told on a moonlit night in August – and the spreading of the nightsoil (even the word is indicative of its use) on the nearest border was to lighten and make more workable the heavy, claggy, limestone 'brash' or clay, which is the naturally occurring soil in this garden. Near the privy, I can grow plants that struggle elsewhere, and I have nothing but gratitude and admiration for those unfastidious cottagers of old.

Further along the path is a disused goose house, whose occupants would once have added to the garden soil, as well as keeping down the grass by grazing. In days gone by, a pig would have been kept and fed on kitchen scraps, adding its own particularly rich manure to the soil. And, of course, ashes from house fires would have found their way on to the garden.

If you feel that this subject is not suitable for a gardening column, you would be wrong. Indeed, it is hard to think of anything more important to a gardener than the fertility and structure of his soil. Soil can make or mar a gardener's designs. The hardest struggle I face is to improve my soil in just a few years, when it took my predecessors decades or more. When I see an old-established village garden disappear under a crowd of new houses, I could weep. This is not because I dislike new houses in villages, far from it, but because of the permanent loss of that hard-won, workable, fertile soil.

Modern-day gardeners, without the benefit of privies or pigs, have learned other ways to improve their soil. Where once the kitchen scraps were recycled through the gut of a pig, they are now put in compost bins, together with garden waste, to degrade and rot into something almost as efficacious. Whole books have been written on the subject, over-complicating it in the process. It is not so difficult, or time-consuming, provided that you have bins at least 1 cubic yard/ metre in volume, and use plenty of well-shredded woody material or cardboard (promoting air circulation and adding carbon) to counter-balance a good mix of soft green vegetable matter. If you like, a little animal manure or sulphate of ammonia can be added to encourage the work rate of the micro-organisms that break down the soil. The bins should be filled as quickly as possible, watered periodically so that the contents are damp, and always covered. If you don't expect that, as a matter of course, the frenetic microbial activity will heat up the heap sufficiently to kill every weed seed, all will be fine.

The gardener's preoccupation (I put it no higher than that) with animal and vegetable waste products, and their putrefaction and degradation, can seem a little weird. But once the rotting process is finished, the result could not be less smelly, harmful or objectionable. Indeed, it is one of life's satisfactions to handle loam-scented, well-rotted compost. However, gardeners commit a serious error of taste when they admit to urinating on their compost heap (urine being a powerful activator). It is not in the same league of disgustingness as using the contents of privies – although distance has a way of lending enchantment to that – but the boastful pleasure gardeners take in admitting to this is, to say the least, offputting.

The making of compost seems to me one of life's essential, taken-for-granted accomplishments, like being able to tie your shoe laces or recite the names of England's 1966 World Cup winning team. This year, however, I have gone even further into the realms of rotting. In the past, I have made leaf mould by putting swept leaves into a double-thickness black plastic bag, and placing it somewhere inconspicuous for two years. The process took that long because it was achieved without oxygen, and slower-working fungi rather than bacteria were the main agents of decay. Last year, however, I erected a simple square structure, consisting of four wooden stakes to which chicken wire was attached. In a single year, without any attention from me, the leaves put in this bin have turned to a delicious, chocolate-brown, friable, leaf mould, marvellous for potting composts as well as a mulch for woodland plants. And, best of all, no urine was required.

The Spectator
December 2005

I have written in the past that gardening is character-forming, and so it is. It can also, however, be character-harming, and I have direct experience of that. Thirty years of gardening, and more than twenty years of writing about it, have changed my character for the worse. I started out life as a sweet, retiring, reticent creature, happy just to be left alone to sow my sweet peas and prune my roses; I am now a Bossy Boots, forever giving my advice, whether it is requested or not. Whenever gardeners congregate, there I will be, holding forth about the need to remove the fruit cage netting in November or the inadvisability of growing yellow conifers in rural situations.

Having a regular public platform does that to you. Ask any journalist. For many years, off and on, in a variety of publications, I have written a Jobs To Do column. There was a time when I (quietly) thought that this kind of column was bossy, and risked undermining the reader and reducing gardening, which I love, to a succession of rather dreary-sounding tasks. But these days I am completely converted, partly because I have developed an overbearing personality, partly because writing these tips serves as an efficient means of jogging my own memory and partly because the columns appear to be very popular with readers. This is not because of my mellifluous prose, since the advice is often pared down to the barest minimum of words that can still convey some kind of meaning, but because it seems that every gardener in the land wants to be reminded what to tackle each Saturday morning.

The suggestions I provide so succinctly are, I am told, extremely useful, particularly for busy people, although I am occasionally greeted by someone at dinner on a Saturday night or after church on Sunday, with the words: 'The ground wasn't right to sow seeds, so I am afraid I just ignored your advice', the subtext being 'So there, smarty-pants'. I may protest that the tips were merely suggestions, but the readers, perhaps rightly, do not believe me.

More often, however, I meet gratitude, and I have to admit that this has quite gone to my head. I now think my opinion is worth hearing on everything from the Conservative leadership contest to the disadvantages of northern hemisphere rugby union back lines standing too flat across the pitch.

The truth is that it is often a toss-up whether, in the finite time you have available for gardening at the weekend, you divide herbaceous perennials or take cuttings of pelargoniums, and my job (I promise) is less to tell you what to do, than simply to help you choose. A problem can arise, it is true, when writing of some tasks, such as pruning apple trees in winter, which have a long time span. This is a job that you can do at any time between late November and early March, yet I feel an understandable reticence about mentioning a task too often during its duration. In any event, there are usually far more jobs pressing than space in which to mention them.

As far as providing these tips is concerned, I am lucky to live in the Midlands. Although my suggestions may sometimes be too advanced for those in Northumberland and (heavens!) occasionally too late for anyone in Devon, they chime with the experience of a great tranche of readers living in lowland areas between the Thames and the Tees. Scottish readers, whom I meet from time to time, take a particular delight in telling me that the timing of my advice is quite useless to them, but they are used to saying that about most gardening advice offered and might, I imagine, miss the opportunity for scorn if I didn't give it to them.

December, however, is when you, the reader, can get your own back. If you find the bossiness unappealing, then simply ignore me. There are plenty of things that I will tell (I mean advise) you to do – net holly berries, plant garlic, prune the grapevine, plant dormant trees, shrubs and roses, for example – but if you don't want to, then don't. Indeed, if the weather is snowy or the ground waterlogged or frozen, even I have to admit that you would be best not doing anything at all. Provided you have already protected any tender plants against the weather, or you couldn't care less either way, everything else can wait. For once, the choice is yours, not mine. So have a happy, guilt-free Christmas. And, for heaven's sake, find something more interesting to do on Boxing Day than sowing your onion seed in trays of seed compost under glass. Whatever I say.

5

PLANTS

'Borderlines', *Daily Telegraph*
9 February 2008

It has surprised me greatly how much keener my powers of observation have become as I have got older, even though my eyesight is worse. I suppose that it comes from increasing experience and knowledge, and it is rather heartening to think that it is the way you look at things that matters. Although I spent a good deal of my childhood out of doors, I cannot remember ever noticing the twigs of any trees in winter, except ash, because of their strange, black triangular buds, stuck at the end of upward-pointing twigs, and horse chestnuts with their large, distinctively sticky buds. Now I am grown up, however, the sight of winter twigs, shorn of their masking leaves, affects me deeply. Indeed, these stems often seem to me one of the great compensations we have for the shortness of the days, the wetness of the soil and the sharpness of the wind, all of which make gardening a mixed pleasure in January and early February.

You don't have to be a gardener, of course, to notice and enjoy the colour of tree stems in winter. In places in the countryside where there are still shaws, by which I mean thickets of trees and shrubs, especially along streams, there will often be the native willow, *Salix alba* var. *vitellina*, with its golden young stems or, if you're lucky, 'Britzensis', which has orange-red ones. On well-grown trees, a mass of these stems will glow like embers in the glancing winter sunshine. In hedgerows, the stems of the native dogwood, *Cornus alba*, are deep purple-red, which sets them startlingly apart from the dour brown branches of the accompanying blackthorn, elder and hawthorn. As for the large-leaved lime, *Tilia platyphyllos*, the young growths look as if they have been dipped in fresh blood.

If you are a gardener, however, there is so much more to enjoy. There is the vast tribe of willows, almost all of which have young stems of a different colour from the older wood. There is *Salix daphnoides*, with its violet stems, not to mention *Salix acutifolia* 'Blue Streak' with blue stems, and a white bloom, as well as silvery buds. Willow stems can be propagated simply by cutting them and putting them in water, until roots begin to appear (which is something I do remember doing in my childhood). And, if you pollard or coppice willows regularly, they never get too big and out of hand. Best of all, used imaginatively, willows can bring such a lot of fun to the garden, in the shape of 'living' crocodiles, chairs, arbours or diaphanous, criss-cross, boundary hedges.

Then there are the ornamental blackberries (*Rubus*), which, admittedly, have a reputation for being thuggish and prickly. However, if cut down every year, they can be controlled and I love the way their young, ghostly white stems loom eerily out of an early morning mist. *Rubus cockburnianus* and *R. thibetanus* are the best known.

Also an asset, for damp soils in large gardens in particular, are the garden forms of the native dogwood, *Cornus alba*, as well as the yellow-green-stemmed *C. sericea* 'Flaviramea', which we used to call *C. stolonifera*. My favourite, however, is the well-behaved *Cornus sanguinea* 'Midwinter Fire'. The base of the young stems are golden but, a third of the way up, they begin to redden, until they are deep scarlet at the tips. The closer and more steadily you observe these plants, the more wonderful they seem to be.

The Spectator
17 March 2007

'Golden Harvest' 1 Y-Y, 'High Society' 2 W-GWP, 'Jetfire' 6 Y-O: these names strangely preoccupy me at this season of the year. If you think that my trolley and I have gone our separate ways, you cannot be *au fait* with the classification of *Narcissus*. If that is the case, I cannot say I exactly blame you, since life is short. However, there is, I assure you, a potent fascination in being able to nail, at a glance, the division to which a particular daffodil belongs.

There is some point in all keen gardeners knowing about *Narcissus* classification, since if you order daffodils from a specialist nursery you will come across these strange compressions. Daffodil breeders have to register their new cultivars in this way with the International Registration Authority, which, since 1955, has been the Royal Horticultural Society, and they find it a useful shorthand when dealing with knowledgeable customers. It assumes, of course, some basic knowledge of botany but, if you are too young to have been taught much of that at school, the basic vocabulary can be picked up quickly enough from the glossaries of terms in plant encyclopaedias.

The genus *Narcissus* is divided into thirteen, the divisions depending on the different form of the flower and/or its origins. Division 1 encompasses all those that have trumpets (strictly speaking coronas), which are at least as long or longer than the outer ring of petals (perianth segments). Division 2 are 'large-cupped', which means that the corona is more than one-third the length of, but not as long as, the perianth. Division 3 are 'small-cupped', Division 4 'double' and so it goes on. A number of the divisions refer to cultivars that can be traced back easily to a particular species; for example, cultivars in Division 6 derive from *Narcissus cyclamineus*, while those in Division 9 from *Narcissus poeticus*. The oddest is Division 11, for 'split-corona' daffodils; these frankly don't look much like daffs at all, since the corona is splayed back against the perianth segments. Division 11 is sub-divided into 'collar', when the corona segments are opposite the perianth segments, and 'papillon', when they alternate. Phew!

The capital letters that follow the division number refer most concisely to the colour(s) of the flower. The first letter is the colour of the perianth, while those after the dash refer to the corona. Y is for yellow, W for white or whitish, G for green, O for orange, P for pink, R for red. Thus 'Golden Harvest' and 'Carlton', planted with such irritating enthusiasm and thoughtlessness wherever a council or over-energetic garden owner can find a virgin stretch of grass, are both 1 Y-Y. (Although last week in Cornwall, on the banks of an old railway line, I was thrilled to come across our native Lent lily, *Narcissus pseudonarcissus* (13 Y-Y), and the centuries-old double 'Telamonus Plenus' (4 Y-Y).) 'High Society' (2W-GWP) is a large-cupped daffodil, with white perianth, and a corona that is green at the base, then white in the mid-zone and pink at the corona rim. 'Jetfire' (6 Y-O) is derived from *N. cyclamineus*, so is to be found in Division 6, and has a yellow perianth and orange corona. Simple and logical, isn't it?

Of course, formal registration of a new cultivated variety requires a great deal more information than this: for example, whether there is one flower or more to the stem; whether the flowers are scented (those of Division 7 which derive from *Narcissus jonquilla* being conspicuously so); whether the corona mouth is even or wavy, frilled or lobed, and the rim flanged or rolled; the breeder's name, date of breeding and parentage of the cultivar. All this information is also likely to be found in specialist catalogues.

The point of this pinpoint classification is simple and compelling. Daffodils, as well as tulips, dahlias, chrysanthemums, rhododendrons and roses, are such enormous genera, and capable of hybridizing so easily to produce new, distinct cultivars, that an internationally recognized register is the only way of keeping a taxonomically accurate grip. Frankly, without definitive names linked to accurate descriptions to depend on, we gardeners would be absolutely sunk, since how else do we know we will get what we ask for? In the tercentenary year of Carl Linnaeus's birth, I feel I owe it to him, not to mention his many plant systematist forebears, to acknowledge the importance of classification and, where possible, to derive pleasure and instruction from it. At the very least, it makes spring car journeys more interesting.

The Spectator
May 2008

In 1811, Jane Austen wrote to her sister, Cassandra, in response, no doubt, to an anxious enquiry: 'I will not say that your mulberry trees are dead, but I am afraid they are not alive.' I know something of how the Blessed Jane felt, for my advice about the health and welfare of mulberry trees is also sometimes sought at this time of year.

The reason is simple. The black mulberry (*Morus nigra*) is one of the last trees to come into leaf in spring. While horse chestnut, sycamore and hazel have fully expanded their leaves, the mulberry is still in tight, discouraging bud. This year, in late April, I looked across my garden at the heavenly apple blossom while the mulberry was resolutely twiggy and bare. No wonder Cassandra Austen was in a panic.

Nor is the mulberry the only one to take things at a leisurely pace. The Indian bean tree (*Catalpa bignonioides*), much loved by gardeners in the suburbs, which has very large, heart-shaped leaves, foxglove flowers and long, stringy bean seedpods, is even slower to green up. Nor should you expect anything until mid-May from the Chinese paperbark maple (*Acer griseum*) either. The Judas tree (*Cercis siliquastrum*) usually starts to produce its purple-pink pea flowers before the leaves unfold in late spring, and is the better for it but, curiously, flowers and leaves have come together this year. In the case of shrubs, hibiscus always looks completely dead until at least the middle of this month, whilst *Edgeworthia chrysantha* and *Magnolia wilsonii* are also liable to fray my nerves.

Although this may seem worrying to us, for the tree or shrub there is a distinct advantage in leafing late, especially if those leaves are large. That way they are likely to escape damage from late spring frosts. Many a hydrangea could learn something from the *festina lente* approach of the mulberry. What is interesting, however, is that the mulberry is also one of the first trees to colour in autumn, and to lose its leaves in the annual fall. The effort of producing prodigal quantities of fruit must exhaust it.

Although some trees, like mulberries, are reliable and consistent late-leafers, a number of others will vary in some degree from year to year. Amongst our native trees, oak and ash are the most famous examples of this. They Box and Cox and, in the process, fox. We all know the nineteenth-century proverb: 'When the oak is before the ash, then you will only get a splash; when the ash is before the oak, then you may expect a soak', which refers to the amount of rain that is likely to follow in the summer. Last year, as I recall, the ash was first and, by golly, we got a soak; this year, in the copse that I planted fifteen years ago, it has been neck and neck between them, so I confidently expect a sploak.

The study of the recurrence of natural phenomena, such as the breaking of tree leaf buds and the appearance of flowers, butterflies, frogspawn and so on in spring, is called phenology. The 'founding father of phenology' was Robert Marsham (1708–97), who lived in Stratton Strawless, Norfolk, through most of the eighteenth century. He studied and listed twenty-seven 'Intimations of Spring' each year from 1736, keeping meticulous records all his long life. His family continued the recording until 1958, a most impressive achievement and an immensely valuable one in times of climate change. It is the 300th anniversary of the birth of Robert Marsham this year, and we should salute him. Stratton Strawless is certainly *en fête* this summer, with a number of events planned to honour his memory and underline the importance of his work.

Marsham was famously knowledgeable about trees, and a great planter of them, so it is permissible to wonder at what date the Marsham mulberries began to leaf in 1811. Jane Austen's letter is dated 31 May and I have to say that, this year, my mulberry tree had fully expanded its leaves by 20 May. Although long hard winters can retard bud-break (and in the early nineteenth century they were certainly colder than those we have experienced in recent years), and ailing trees of any kind also tend to be slower than usual, I think we can safely assume that Jane was telling her sister the unwelcome news as kindly as possible. I like to think that, even two centuries later, we gardeners can sympathize readily with this small domestic sadness.

The Spectator
May 2006

It is an intriguing fact that, every half-century or so, a conifer arrives on the scene which makes a real impact on our gardens. (As every schoolchild knows, a conifer is a cone-bearing gymnospermous and exogenous tree, usually, although not invariably, with an evergreen habit.)

In 1853, the giant redwood (*Sequoiadendron giganteum*) was introduced from California, and was an immediate hit. Its name was changed to wellingtonia to honour the Duke of Wellington, who had died the year before. This tree was planted widely in country house gardens and in public parks, and is sufficiently tall to be picked out from a distance even now. The wood is red, and the bark soft and easily battered.

In the early 1890s, a chance cross between two conifers, *Cupressus macrocarpa* and *Chamaecyparis nootkatensis*, resulted in a hybrid tree of great vigour, grown first at Haggerston Hall in Northumberland by a man called Leyland.

This was named by botanists × *Cupressocyparis leylandii*. The Leyland cypress has proved such a fast-growing, potentially tall, hedging plant that it is feared and loathed by house owners all over the country, who find themselves at the mercy of their privacy-loving or just plain stroppy neighbours.

During the Second World War, a deciduous conifer, *Metasequoia glyptostroboides*, known until then only from fossil records, was discovered in a remote locality on the borders of Hupeh and Sechuan in China. At the end of the war, seed was sent to the Arnold Arboretum in Massachusetts, whence in 1948 it was widely distributed to gardens in the temperate world, including the British Isles. Gardeners planted this tree with bated breath, since no one had any idea how easy or difficult it would be to grow. One old gardener told me that 'We practically took its temperature every night.' But the metasequoia has turned out to be hardy, easy and fast growing, without being overbearing, and is a significant feature now in many a large garden. It has a steeply tapering, deeply fissured trunk, and pleasant emerald-green leaves, which turn pinkish-brown before falling in autumn.

Now, fifty years later, it is the turn of Australia to get in on the act, with the discovery of the Wollemi pine (*Wollemia nobilis*), in the Wollemi National Park, 125 miles/200 kilometres west of Sydney. The discoverer was an intrepid parks officer called David Noble who, on 10 September 1994, found a stand of trees, after abseiling down into an immensely remote and deep rainforest gorge. There are fossil records of this tree, 90 million years old, but fewer than 100 mature trees have so far been found in the gorge – and nowhere else. The largest tree is 130 feet/40 metres tall, the oldest probably about a thousand years old. The Director of the Royal Botanic Gardens, Sydney, pronounced that the discovery was the equivalent of finding a small dinosaur alive. Which prompts one to send up a prayer of thanks that trees can't move.

The tree has pendulous, dark green foliage, not unlike a fir, but with softer needles, and bubbly, dark brown bark. It is in the *Araucaria* family, its nearest relatives being the monkey puzzle tree from Chile and the Norfolk Island pine from the Pacific. It is reputedly hardy down to 23°F/–5°C, so is a realistic prospect for gardens in the south and west, and has already been planted at, *inter alia*, Kew, the Eden Project, Trentham Gardens, Westonbirt, Bowood and Tregothanan, and also, to get more idea of its cold tolerance, at the RHS Garden at Harlow Carr in Yorkshire.

Mike Nelhams, the irrepressible Curator of Tresco Abbey Gardens on the Isles of Scilly (which has a good claim to be the finest of all sub-tropical gardens in this country), told me how he acquired his tree. Lord Phillimore, who was born on Tresco, rang him up late last year to say that he had bid successfully for a Wollemi pine at the auction held by Sotheby's in Sydney of the first 200 propagated trees, organized to raise money for the tree's conservation, and that he wished to donate it to Tresco Abbey Gardens. Mike drove to Kew to collect it, and strapped it carefully into the car to take it home. 'It was better than having a blonde in the passenger seat.' Quite so. Tresco's Wollemi pine was planted last week, close to its rare relatives, *Araucaria excelsa* and *Agathis australis*. Mike says that he won't put his plant in a cage, to deter thieves, 'since no one could carry anything off Tresco without the whole island knowing'.

In fact, from this month on, anyone can lend a hand in conserving it. Even flat dwellers, since, like the Norfolk Island pine, the Wollemi pine can be grown as a container plant indoors. Plants are now commercially available for £97 from the sole British distributors, Kernock Park Plants in Cornwall, in a 3-litre pot (16–18 inches/40–45 centimetres high), to be delivered in late summer. For those who cannot wait that long, there are a few 5-litre pot plants (24–26 inches/60–65 centimetres high) available now at £300; these were grown in Australia and flown here. Well, what are we waiting for?

The Spectator
June 2004

It is said that people often catch divorce from their friends, as if it were an infectious disease. It is certainly true that gardeners catch plants from their neighbours. Although this is hardly as harmful to all concerned, it can certainly be a disadvantage, at least to the impartial observer. *Robinia* 'Frisia', *Spiraea* 'Goldflame' and 'Castlewellan' Leyland cypress all break out from time to time in a district, like a dose of yellow fever. Worst of all, in my opinion, however, is an epidemic of the double pink ornamental cherry *Prunus* 'Kanzan'.

At the end of April, my husband and I spent a sunny weekend on the north Norfolk coast. It was marvellous spring weather for walking on the edge of salt marshes, looking at birds. Occasionally we would turn inland to take in a picturesque village (of which there are many) for the purposes of church and pub visiting – usually in that order. The village gardens were looking wonderful: lushly green, full of bright tulips and spring promise. But in far, far too many of them, especially those belonging to 'done up' houses, there was one of these wretched cherry trees. Indeed, in all my years of shivering convulsively at the sight of 'Kanzan', I never remember a weekend of such continuous tremor.

Even if you do not know the name, I am sure you will recognize the description. 'Kanzan' is the stiff-branched, vase-shaped cherry tree with copper-bronze young leaves appearing at the same time as extravagantly double, silly, frilly, purplish-rose flowers. It has some orange autumn leaf colour, true, but nowhere like as good as *Prunus sargentii*, say. Because the flowers are double, there are, of course, no cherries for the birds, and the branches spread towards the horizontal only in the tree's later years.

'Kanzan' is one, indeed the most famous probably, of the Sato Zakura, the collective name for Japanese garden cherries, that race of revered trees bred over centuries in Japan, but whose origins are now mistily obscure. A few, such as 'Taihaku' or 'Shirotae' (both white), are trees of great personality and charm. 'Kanzan' has personality in spades, but its lumpy flowers are decidedly short on charm. Its offspring, 'Pink Perfection', is a better bet, having clearer pink flowers and less bronzey leaves.

W.J. Bean, whose pre-war *Trees and Shrubs Hardy in the British Isles* (4 vols) is still widely consulted by thoughtful gardeners, damned *Prunus* 'Kanzan' with generous praise in 1933. 'The most widely planted of the Sato Zakura,' he wrote, 'and understandably so, for it is of excellent constitution, very free-flowering and of the right habit for street-planting. Its only fault, apart from the impure pink of its flowers, is that in gardens it usurps the place of other cherries of more charm and character, and that it is too often planted in country districts, where it is grossly out of place in the spring landscape.' Too right, old Bean. In a countryside so full of natural, understated, beauty as north Norfolk, what possesses people to overlay it with these stiff-necked trees and flowers the colour of cheap strawberry ice-cream?

Sure, 'Kanzan' is of vigorous constitution but, as with most Japanese cherries, if planted in a lawn, as it so often is, the roots annoyingly run just under, or even over, the surface of the grass, making mowing a positive torture. It is also susceptible to bacterial canker, cherry leaf scorch and silver leaf, although in that regard it is no different from any other prunus.

Why do Norfolk village gardeners catch the contagion of this tree from their neighbours? In countless cottage gardens, which until quite recently would have been graced by useful, homely 'Bramley' or 'Norfolk Beefing' apple trees, with their wonderful April pinkish-white blossom, this interloper pokes its gawky limbs above many a fine – and expensively renovated – brick and flint wall. Even if the 'Bramley' no longer seems suitable, why not a soberer ornamental crab apple (*Malus*), which is much less prone to disease than prunus, or even a fruitful quince tree (*Cydonia*), such as 'Meech's Prolific'? (My quince trees all came from that excellent Norfolk nursery Read's of Loddon, the other side of Norwich – hardly too far a journey for the Ssangyong Musso 4 × 4, I should have thought.)

The only mercy is that this prunus, like most other Japanese cherries, is not long lived. Forty years is a good span, fifty if you are unlucky. So those 'Kanzan' cherries, which were planted when north Norfolk was gentrified some twenty years ago, are roughly half way through their span. It is unwise to replant a cherry with another, so the question inevitably arises, what will these gardens go down with next?

'Borderlines', *Daily Telegraph*
2 July 2005

If you were to compile a list of over-used words – those that have almost lost their meaning because they are used so indiscriminately – 'indispensable' would surely be, well, indispensable. The dictionary definition is 'absolutely necessary'. Honestly, how many things in life are that?

When I really consider the matter, I cannot think of that many plants in the garden which are truly indispensable. Useful, beautiful, eminently desirable, sure, but not indispensable. By indispensable, I mean (and probably you do, too) that I could not contemplate making a garden without them; plants, in fact, with such character, personality and beauty, such unfussy sturdiness and uncomplaining amiability, that life simply wouldn't be as good without them.

For me, hornbeam would have to be one of these, since hedges are 'absolutely necessary' in my windy garden. Hornbeam will grow on heavy clay soil, which I have in parts of the garden, and it retains its leaves in winter, if I trim it in July. I really do not think I could do without life-enhancing daffodils, tulips and irises in spring, either, nor yet in June the rose 'Madame Alfred Carrière', for its associations with my childhood and its delicious scent of tinned lychees. I grow it up the tennis court boundary netting, and it consoles me for my rotten backhand, every time I go to the back of the court. I could not consider a fruit garden without a quince tree, for the pale pink flowers in May and the heavy yellow fruits hanging from the boughs in autumn. And, in the border, I should be a fool ever to try to do without *Aster × frikartii* 'Mönch', a Michaelmas daisy which flowers continuously from August until October and has rough-to-the-touch, mildew-proof leaves and strong stems topped by clusters of single, bluish-mauve flowers with yellow eyes. These are flowers which seem to blend successfully with anything and everything.

Right at this moment, there is a plant which every day catches my heart with its curvilinear grace, its airy charm and singularity, and my mind with its neatness, reliability and usefulness. It is *Helictotrichon sempervirens*, an evergreen, hardy, clump-forming grass which sends up straw-coloured panicles, which nod at the tips, in a diaphanous fountain spray in May and June. One minute it is a well-behaved, 18-inch/45-centimetre-high hummock of thin, slightly twisted, spear-like leaves; the next it has erupted into exuberant life. The leaves are evergreen only in the sense that they endure through the winter; they are actually steely blue in colour and the perfect foil for zingy orange Oriental poppies.

It being easy to propagate, I simply dig up bits and divide them in spring or early autumn, and place it where the soil is lightest and the light best. It has become a kind of *leitmotif*, providing a unifying component to plantings in sunny borders around the garden. In early summer it flowers, in late summer it has biscuity seed heads and on frosty winter mornings it cheers me when the hoar has silvered the glaucous leaves. Indispensable? Yes, after due consideration, I think so.

The Spectator

August 2007

Depending on whether you are a housewife, Lothario or a gardener, 'bedding' can mean a number of different things. As a horticultural term, it dates from the early decades of the nineteenth century, when adventurous Victorian head gardeners, especially those working on large private estates, began to use large numbers of low-growing tender plants, to create a colourful, exuberant display on terraces and parterres.

These tender perennials and annuals (mainly from the frost-free regions of South America and South Africa) – calceolarias, pelargoniums, lobelias, salvias, petunias, African marigolds and the like – were grown from seed in heated glasshouses and 'bedded out' in late May or early June. They did not survive the frosts in October, so the custom grew up of replacing them then with hardy biennial flowers and bulbs for display in spring. Costly in time and labour, this practice was a persuasive means of emphasizing the wealth of a landowner.

The custom soon trickled down to private gardens, where 'a nice splash of colour' appealed to those who favoured the 'gardenesque' style. Public authorities saw the point as well, and bedding out has remained, in simplified form, a feature of parks and public spaces to this day. The effects are consciously crowd-pleasing, and designed, as they were in private gardens, to be viewed from a distance.

The habit of bedding out has endured remarkably well. Those who do not care to use half-hardies to create blocks of distinct colours nevertheless often employ them to fill those gaps which appear in borders from time to time, and to enhance the effect of hardy perennials in the summer garden. For myself, I grow a number from seed each year (a rather old-fashioned and expensive way of doing it but it gives me the choice I would not find otherwise) in order to ginger up my summer plantings. Favourites include *Nicotiana langsdorffii*, *Rudbeckia* 'Prairie Sun', *Tithonia rotundifolia* and *Verbena rigida*.

These days, it is true, half-hardy annuals are mainly planted in containers of one sort or another: tubs, pots, half-barrels and hanging baskets. In the pots and urns that I have placed to emphasize doorways or steps, I grow a range of the cleaner-coloured petunias, such as cascading 'Blue Wave', as well as the yellow-flowered *Bidens* 'Golden Goddess' and a number of marguerites (*Argyranthemum*). Despite their tolerance of shade, I don't grow the oh-so-popular busy Lizzies (*Impatiens*) because of their repelling colours and flat, fleshy, mildly creepy foliage.

It is possible that most readers have never planted up a hanging basket, since, suspended and unconnected, these look ridiculous in a garden setting. But they will certainly know them from the pubs they enter and the lamp posts they pass in the more self-respecting of our towns and suburbs. And, should they go into a garden centre in late spring, they cannot fail to notice that most of the planteria will be given over to small pots or 'plugs' of half-hardies, many with habits suitable for containers. For the convenience of customers, these may already be planted out in large plastic containers and hanging baskets.

Plant breeders make strenuous efforts to develop strains of annuals, which will fulfil the most important criteria that the growers and retailers require: colour impact, compact growth, a free-flowering habit, weather resistance and trueness from seed (since it is more expensive to raise these plants from cuttings). The garden centres strive equally strenuously to make the business less complicated, in order to extract the 'leisure pound' from the horticulturally disengaged. The better sort of garden centre will even attempt to show customers what colour and habit combinations will look well together, in 'recipes' that take away the guesswork altogether. Instead of selling 'mixtures' of flower colour, there is a welcome move towards promoting colour-themed packages of plants.

Every year, I visit the open-air trial grounds of seedsmen, to inform myself as to what new varieties, even genera, they will be introducing to gardeners (how many people grew angelonias, bacopas or dichondras ten years ago?). I also look at those which do well in garden conditions each year, and note those which I might be tempted to grow in my garden.

This summer has been particularly instructive. One trial ground had been flooded for several days but the only annuals that looked really sick were *Nicotiana* and *Impatiens*. The largest-flowered petunias were ragged, but the new, smaller-flowered 'Shock Wave' varieties were wonderfully floriferous and almost rainproof, as they have been in my garden this summer. The plant, however, which has stood both the heat of last summer, and the cool, humid, damp conditions of this, is the orange-red, pendulous-flowered, fleshy-leaved *Begonia* 'Million Kisses'. So it's just a great pity that, like quite a lot of half-hardies, it does not go with anything and it isn't very pretty.

'Borderlines', *Daily Telegraph*
1 September 2007

Beth Chatto has called it 'absolutely the best Michaelmas daisy for long display and sheer beauty' while the late Graham Stuart Thomas maintained that 'during this long period [of flowering] there are few plants which can hold a candle to it'. What is this plant, which attracts such admiration from the best plantsmen of our day? The answer is *Aster* × *frikartii* 'Mönch', an elegant daisy which starts to flower in late July or early August and keeps going until late September or even early October, when the baton is finally passed to the true Michaelmas daisies.

We should all be very grateful to *Aster* × *frikartii* 'Mönch'. At a time of year when most roses have lost their vim, hardy chrysanthemums are still only in tight green bud and the summer-flowering grasses are in need of a foil to show them off to best advantage, this hardy perennial has become precious to all gardeners who wish to paint seasonal pictures in their borders.

The story of *Aster × frikartii* goes back over a hundred years, to a time soon after the Himalayan species *Aster thomsonii* was introduced into this country. A talented and energetic clergyman called the Reverend Charles Wolley-Dod (after whom a rose is named) saw the potential of crossing this long-flowering, reasonably short-growing aster with *Aster amellus*, the Italian starwort, which had been grown in this country for three centuries, was taller than *A. thomsonii* but flowered for a much shorter period in summer. Both were resistant to mildew, the curse which besets *Aster novi-belgii* cultivars. Wolley-Dod raised seedlings of *Aster × frikartii*, which he exhibited to the Royal Horticultural Society in 1892, and then – nothing. Somehow, they were lost. Fortunately, a Swiss nurseryman called Frikart made the same cross at his nursery at Stäfa, and had raised three seedlings by 1918, naming them, charmingly, after Alps: 'Mönch', 'Eiger' and 'Jungfrau'. In 1924, he added 'Wunder von Stäfa'.

Over the years, there has been much disputation about the differences, or lack of them, between 'Mönch' and 'Wunder von Stäfa', especially because they can show variation in height and colour, depending where they are grown, even in the same garden. I turned to Paul Picton, who holds the National Collection of asters at his Old Court Nurseries, for an authoritative word on the subject. He believes that 'Wunder von Stäfa' is identical to 'Mönch' in flower shape, size and colour, but it is shorter growing, at 30 inches/75 centimetres tall, so does not need staking. According to the *RHS Plant Finder*, 'Mönch' is rare in gardens and most of the plants on sale are 'Wunder von Stäfa'. I bought mine as 'Mönch' and I do believe that is what it is, for it grows to 39 inches/100 centimetres tall, and it definitely needs support.

My plant has thin but reasonably sturdy stems; from each arise a number of side shoots, on the end of which is a single flower, with a diameter of 2 inches/6 centimetres. The ray florets are thin, and a cool, refined lavender-blue in colour, and begin to curl and twist as they age, while the disc florets in the centre of the flowers are bright yellow. Now that the clumps are well established, they are a wonderful sight, beckoning to me from across the garden.

Aster × *frikartii* likes an alkaline and well-drained soil. Clay soils should definitely be lightened with grit. Although this plant is happiest in sun, and is quite drought-tolerant, I have a clump also in a north-facing border, which makes rather greener leaves, is shorter in stem and flowers more sparsely. *Aster* × *frikartii* needs to be divided only every four or five years, a task which should always be done in early spring, when also softwood cuttings can be taken. Otherwise, apart from some discreet staking, it requires no maintenance. Deadheading is pointless, says Paul, because there is not enough time for it to make buds for a second flush and, in any event, this aster has attractive, small, fluffy seed heads, which the birds may like in autumn and early winter.

The flowers associate beautifully with other summer daisies, such as the yellow-flowered *Rudbeckia* 'Goldsturm' (which picks up on the yellow centres of the daisy) and also with the shorter grasses, like *Stipa tenuissima*. Paul Picton also likes to grow this plant behind *Sedum* 'Autumn Joy', which is sturdy enough not to mind if the aster flops over it. I grow it close to the continuous-flowering, golden-yellow English Rose 'Graham Thomas'; the fact that the great man thought 'Mönch' one of the six best garden plants makes this a charming coincidence.

'Borderlines', *Daily Telegraph*
16 September 2006

While on holiday in Norfolk at the end of June, my husband and I decided to visit the gardens at Mannington Hall. They are particularly famous for their roses and we were there just at the right moment in the season to see the finest display. We arrived, as good luck would have it, just in time to join a tour being conducted by the owner, Lord Walpole. Almost immediately he stopped at a grove of three gum trees (*Eucalyptus gunnii*). He encouraged us – a group of middle-aged, deeply respectable, reticent couples by the look of things – to press our ears to the trunks of the trees and listen to them 'gurgle'. Doubtingly, but politely, since we did not wish to disappoint a peer, who was looking on like a benign Gandalfian magician, we did so, only for my husband to jump like a scalded cat when he heard what he described as 'a surprisingly loud noise'. Despite several attempts, I heard nothing, although several others obviously did. This was a subject never raised in my structural botany classes at Kew, so I asked Lord Walpole how he knew. He said that a forestry expert had let him in on the secret, but that he personally had only had success listening to young eucalypts, although he believed that it was possible with young London planes as well.

There is no doubt that, whether we hug them or not, most of us feel a great admiration, even awe, of trees. Eminent writers, such as Thomas Pakenham, have tapped into this secular worship of trees. The latest arboreal publicist is Colin Tudge, whose quite brilliant book *The Secret Life of Trees* has recently come out in paperback. Colin Tudge is a hero in everything but name; he is both scientist and philosopher, which is probably why he views trees in such an original way.

He also writes beautifully. This is his description of the aspen: 'It has a languid air, with wanly fluttering leaves on long flat stalks, which in autumn turn a melancholic yellow . . . Yet for all its bloodless foppishness, the quaking aspen has the widest distribution of any North American tree . . . How come?' Apparently, because of its ability to bounce back after fire, since it suckers so freely. Well, I never.

After my Mannington experience, I was agog to know Colin Tudge's views on the 'transpiration stream'. He is magisterial: '. . . water is not pumped from below but dragged from above by the leaves, up through the vessels of the xylem, not in a crude and turbulent gush but in millions on millions of orderly threads. Each liquid thread is only as thick as the bore of the conducting vessels; the biggest are 400 microns across (0.4 of a millimetre) and most are far smaller than this. The tension within them is enormous: the threads are taut as piano wires.' Unfortunately, as far as eucalyptus gurgling is concerned, this is not entirely helpful; indeed, one might have to conclude that the gurgle is an arboreal aberration, though a rather charming one. Perhaps Colin Tudge could enlighten us in the next edition. There are at least three people I can think of who would love to know the answer.

The Spectator
September 2004

It has been rotten weather for gardening here, so far. Rain in late April, too hot weather in early June, then cold nights, drizzle and cloud, followed by furious winds in early July, and torrential rain and flooding in early August. More than 6 inches/15 centimetres of rain have fallen this month, three times the average for this district. A number of shrubs of Mediterranean origin are dying before my eyes, having been submerged in water for three days. Since the garden is set to open on Bank Holiday Monday in aid of church funds, this has plunged me in gloom.

As I look around my sodden, bedraggled, weedy garden, I thank goodness, however, that my livelihood depends on it only tangentially. Indeed, it is possible for me to earn money by moaning publicly about it. But what of all the commercial horticultural operations, whose customers are as sensitive to the weather as I am? I cannot help but sympathize with the thousands of garden centres and nurseries trying to turn a profit in such a climatically challenging year.

Small-scale specialist nurseries, in particular, get my sympathy. Often run by husband and wife teams, with a bit of help, they are usually to be found down some country lane in a distant shire. Some only sell plants on site, while others are solely mail-order businesses, and still more do both. Many were founded in response to the growth of garden centres.

The garden centre, as an idea, was imported from the United States more than forty years ago, when the development of 'containerization' made it viable. Nurserymen discovered that they could display plants in light, plastic pots at any time of year, rather than having to grow them in fields and lift them only in autumn or spring, and so could sell them in retail outlets rather than largely by mail order. (I remember vividly, when I was working for a nursery in Holland in 1976, the frozen-fingered misery of digging perennials out of semi-frozen ground in March, and then having to stand in an almost equally cold and draughty shed to pack them for dispatch to customers.)

Containerization, and the growth of garden centres, transformed and modernized the nursery stock industry and put garden making within the reach of everybody. It did not necessarily suit the most discerning gardeners, however. The quantity of plant varieties that these concerns carried dropped markedly, in part to accommodate more immediately lucrative and less problematic garden items, such as sun loungers and barbecues. There was more emphasis on plants whose main virtue was that they flowered or looked good when young, and so had immediate appeal for casual, 'impulse' buyers.

Most nurseries either became retail garden centres and gave up growing, or became wholesale concerns supplying those centres. As a result, specialist retail nurseries sprang up to serve that part of the gardening public dissatisfied with the new ways of doing things. While garden centres are able to carry a reasonable range of hardy and indoor plants, provided that these are easy and amenable, most do not provide catalogues or stock lists, which makes them all but useless for anyone planning a garden systematically. No one designs their garden and then takes the list of plants required to the local garden centre – or not if they want to be spared teeth-grinding frustration, at least.

In 1987, the fortunes of small-scale nurseries were boosted by the founding of the annually published *Plant Finder* (now the *RHS Plant Finder*), which lists the names of most plants available in this country, and which nurseries sell them. In the 1990s, further help came with the advent of Internet shopping. The tiniest nursery in the furthest corner of the land now has a website, more swiftly and easily updated than any catalogue and with the capacity to reach a worldwide clientele. Ask a search engine for the most abstruse plant you can think of and it will throw up half a dozen nursery websites across the world, most of which will take credit cards.

I am deeply attached to specialist nurseries: for the expertise of the enthusiasts that run them and their generosity in sharing it; for the reasonable price of the plants; and for the luxury of a catalogue. Within driving distance, I can call on Wootten's Plants of Wenhaston for pelargoniums and perennials, Wingwell Nursery near Oakham for perennials, Bluebell Nursery near Ashby de la Zouch for unusual trees and shrubs, Stone House Cottage Nurseries near Kidderminster for climbers and wall plants, the Cottage Herbery near Tenbury Wells for herbs, Claire Austin at Shifnal for irises and peonies, and Field House Nurseries at Gotham near Nottingham for primulas and auriculas. After such a disappointing season, and with a border to plant up this autumn, I'm taking to the roads, or rather country lanes, to fill the boot with good-sized, healthy, interesting plants for £200 or so. This is consoling retail therapy and I need it – just as much as the nurseries need me.

'Borderlines', *Daily Telegraph*
23 October 2004

The Reverend Sydney Smith's idea of heaven was to eat *pâté de fois gras* to the sound of trumpets. Mine is to spend a warm, June day with my nose buried deep in a bloom of the rose 'Evelyn', while a soft breeze blows. Whenever people ask me to name my favourite shrub rose, which they do from time to time, the answer is usually 'Evelyn' (although it can sometimes be 'Graham Thomas', sometimes 'Souvenir du Docteur Jamain', depending on mood). Its soft apricot, full-petalled, large flowers in late June, as well as a strong fruity scent and a highly creditable, long-lasting second flush, seem to me almost everything a rose should, or ever could, be.

'Evelyn' is one of the English Roses bred by David Austin at Albrighton in the west Midlands. This is the strain of shrub roses – derived from crossing old roses with Hybrid Teas and Floribundas – which have become such a feature of our gardens in the last thirty years. Their principal characteristics are the beauty of the flower shapes and the deliciousness of the scents, both derived from the old roses, together with repeat-flowering and healthy foliage, which they get from the HTs.

'Evelyn' has large, shallow flowers with numerous petals which gradually recurve to form a rosette shape, as the brochure puts it, and a wonderful peachy fragrance. This is reminiscent of the 'Peregrine' fruits growing on the south-facing wall just behind the rose, when the sun has been on them.

According to Michael Marriott of David Austin Roses, however, 'Evelyn' is no longer considered one of their best roses, because of the slightly sparse growth, and the fact that the large heads of flower can be too heavy for the stems to hold up well. He rather favours 'Sweet Juliet', a stronger-growing rose, with medium-sized flowers of similar colouring but a more, zingy, lemony scent. I have that growing close by, and I admire it greatly, but it is the scent of

'Evelyn' which just gives it the edge for me. Michael, as a good nurseryman, encouraged me to consider trying one of the newest introductions from the David Austin stable, like 'Harlow Carr' or 'Rosemoor', but, outstanding as they undoubtedly are, they are pink, not apricot, and would not fit into my planting scheme.

As autumn advances, 'Evelyn' has finally packed up for the season, with the last buds failing to open properly. In years gone by, I would have felt almost bereft; but not this year, thanks to an unexpected revelation last summer. I was hosting a significant birthday party (a party for a significant birthday, that is, for only others can say how significant the party was). Amongst the presents which I had sternly enjoined the guests not to bring were some Crabtree and Evelyn soaps and shower gel, called 'Evelyn Rose'. It was a gift from some kind, if disobedient, Cumbrian friends and pure serendipity, for I am sure I had never mentioned my affection for this rose. I recalled to mind that David Austin, in 1991, had named the rose 'Evelyn' in honour of the perfumiers Crabtree and Evelyn, and that they had managed, by some alchemy, to distil the scent of the rose and put it into their products. So, as autumn draws on, and the last tattered rose petals flutter to the ground, I have some consolation – and a better excuse than usual to lie about in the bath.

'Borderlines', *Daily Telegraph*
20 November 2004

'Oh good, they've died,' I thought, and then burst out laughing. It suddenly seemed bizarre to be pleased that several sun-loving sub-shrubs and perennials (nepeta, santolina, variegated sages, phlomis, ballota), which were growing in planting pockets on the paved terrace, should all have turned up their toes this autumn, having been immersed in flood water for three days in August.

In fact, I am not really glad, for I like them all. It is just that I am one of those gardeners who often sees plant deaths as opportunities rather than disasters. Especially if the deaths occur in the sunniest, hottest, most favoured part of the garden, where there is never enough space for all the plants that I should like to grow.

Until now, there has been no space for sun-loving desirables like *Nepeta subsessilis* or *Libertia ixioides*, *Incarvillea mairei* or *Tulipa aucheriana*. Now, I find myself doodling with names such as *Seriphidium fragrans* and *Salvia darcyi*, plants that are harder to find than santolina or nepeta, but which will combine to give the terrace a slightly different look for the next few years.

It is a truism that the best gardeners are ruthless ones, happy to pitch out anything that doesn't quite do. I can honestly say, however, that I am as fluffy as a bunny, without a ruthless bone in my body (and by implication, of course, not one of the best gardeners) so the flooding has provided me with an opportunity I simply would not have created for myself. Much as I like *Ballota* 'All Hallow's Green' and *Salvia* 'Icterina', however, sometimes one simply wants a change. Things are unlikely to be much better, just slightly different, that's all.

Of course, there are gardeners who see a death in the garden almost as a personal affront, and wring their hands wondering what on earth they have done to deserve such a calamity. They really should relax. Sometimes, there is a very obvious reason, it's true. Flooding asphyxiates roots, and is as direct and immediate a threat to a plant's well-being as holding a pillow over my face would be to mine. Weather is certainly the biggest killer of plants, and its effects (frost without a blanket of snow in December, say, or bitterly cold drying winds in March) are often sufficiently delayed in their effect to fool us. But pests and diseases can also see off plants, especially if they are very young or very old; again, as in the case of honey fungus, for example, the culprit may not be immediately obvious and you have to go searching for it.

Sometimes, however, plants just die because their time has come to die.

There is a huge variation between species in this regard. Natives have the edge, of course. We all know of ancient, millennarian yew trees, and long-lived lime trees, both species which are well adapted to climate and soil. Exotic trees and shrubs, especially those derived from only a few clones, and those which are fast-growing when young, have a much shorter span. Ceanothus, for example, will give you fifteen years' pleasure, if you are lucky. Of course, if you are not that interested in gardening, a great big hole in a border is a flaming nuisance, requiring a reluctant trip to the garden centre. For the rest of us, it is the chance to introduce one of the very many desirable plants that so far have eluded us.

'Borderlines', *Daily Telegraph*
26 November 2005

As the garden gradually winds down for the winter, there seems to be more time to reflect on the ups and downs of the season, the combinations that have worked and those that have not, and the plants that have made the greatest impression. I often find it is not always the most beautiful, scented or fleeting plants that tug at the memory, but, rather disconcertingly, the plain bizarre. The prize for most memorable plant in my garden this year has gone to *Helianthus salicifolius*, the willow-leaved sunflower, a prairie plant native to the south-central region of the United States.

By anybody's reckoning, this is an extraordinary plant, especially for a windswept prairie. It grows up to 8 feet/2.5 metres tall and needs to be stoutly staked in my garden. It is an herbaceous perennial that grows quickly, its ultra-narrow, linear, willow-like leaves falling away from the broad, round growing tip so that it looks like an out-of-control green Catherine wheel whooshing skywards, or a great green jellyfish pushing up through the sea. Several stems grew from the one crown that I had planted, and at least two of these were badly fasciated, as if several stems had fused together. Fasciation is a random affliction of plants, caused by any number of factors, but usually weather, insect or mechanical damage, or bacterial attack. It always makes a plant look rather weird.

I waited all summer for the flowers to open. Eventually, when September was just ending, they unfurled themselves in a great golden-yellow flourish of single, rayed flowers with brown florets in the middle. By early November, these were over. I gather that this plant will spread using rhizomes and can become invasive, so I plan to plant it out in my 'meadow' next spring, just to see how this hefty perennial, supposedly at home on the prairie, fares in my richer soil. My guess is that it will fall flat on its face, but I'll give it a try.

Some years ago, when I was a young, recently qualified gardener, I saw this plant for the first time on a July day in the garden of a Very Famous Gardener. It was too early in the year for it to be flowering, so there were no very obvious clues to its identity. We stopped in front of it. It was plainly a Talking Point. The VFG asked me if I knew what it was. I shifted from foot to foot in an agony of embarrassment, my brain having turned to gelatine. There was an amused silence for several moments, then the VFG said: 'Hmmph, and I thought you said you were Kew trained.'

It is perhaps not surprising that it has taken more than twenty years for me to bring myself to grow this sunflower in my garden. But, despite the late flowers, the height of the stems and the tendency towards fasciation, I am glad I have. After all, not everything in the garden necessarily has to be lovely. Sometimes, even if you are not a VFG, you need a talking point.

The Spectator
December 2005

I have been in denial for years – I realize that now. I refused to believe that I was a grower of cacti and succulents until one dreary afternoon in early December, when I went into the heated greenhouse, and experienced a sudden and unexpected shock of pleasure at the sight of a lithops in flower. Oh no! I had become a cactus and succulent fancier.

For some years, I have been cultivating (although 'maintaining' has always seemed to me a more accurate word) a number of cactus and succulent plants: rebutias, echeverias, lithops, mammillarias, haworthias, astrophytums, schlumbergeras. Some of these were survivors from early and futile attempts to encourage my children to grow plants; the rest I have bought on those occasions when I have interviewed cactus nurserymen, since it seems impolite to go away empty-handed and, anyway, the plants look rather sweet when small and growing in neat, square, gravel-topped pots. I do very little for them, except resist the temptation to water them for six months between September and March, keep a weather eye out for vine weevil and very, very occasionally repot them. Yet so amenable are they that, despite this neglectful care, they have lived on, slowly multiplying and, every so often, breaking out into marvellous flower. These random-seeming flowerings take me entirely by surprise. For most of the year, *Lithops helmutii*, for example, has squat pairs of fleshy, fat, green and marbled leaves (hence the common name for the genus, 'living stones') but, in autumn or early winter, yellow, white-centred daisy flowers suddenly erupt from the fissure between the leaves. *Lithops* species come from semi-desert in the northern Cape of South Africa and there is something very appealing, even awe-inspiring, about plants that have evolved to mimic their surroundings so closely.

Cactus and succulent growing has always seemed to me (I am ashamed to admit my snobbery) an anorakish pursuit, more about compiling a great long list of disparate species, not capable of providing a convincing, integrated effect – unless you landscape your greenhouse as if it were a small part of the Mohave desert, that is. What this stupid, pointless snobbery blinded me to was the beauty, botanical fascination and variety in the individual species – even those which look too phallic at first sight for sober contemplation.

It was quite uncomfortable, therefore, to discover my closet passion; it produced a painful collision between fact and self-image. We none of us can stand the blinding light of too much reality in our lives, and I had always considered myself an outdoor gardener, almost as deadly a scourge to tender plants as vine weevil. I can be relied upon to kill off houseplants, if called to look after them for any length of time, so my indoor gardening these days is limited to growing forced hyacinths for winter display. For me, the pleasure in gardening has always resided principally in being out in the fresh air and sunlight amongst good, solid, hardy garden plants.

And yet, and yet . . . When I entered the greenhouse that December day, I had to stretch past a score of streptocarpus and pelargoniums in rude health and flower, as well as pots of South African bulbs, a citrus tree with a couple of very promising young lemons, a massive banana plant and tender marguerites by the dozen (brought in to shelter from the stormy blast), in order to pick up the lithops pot to examine it more closely. So, not only am I a cactus fancier, and didn't realize it, but it appears I have also been a long-time greenhouse enthusiast as well. (In fact, I have to own up to possessing two greenhouses, one heated to a minimum winter night-time temperature of 45°F/7°C and one simply insulated with bubble polythene to keep the worst of the frost out.)

So it is high time to come clean and admit that the appeal of the greenhouse is compelling, and particularly so at this time of year. For, when the weather is bleak, there is a special pleasure in being inside looking out, sowing a pot of seed here, removing a botrytis-affected leaf there, or simply dreaming away an afternoon, looking at seed catalogues and making lists – and even examining closely, with the help of a hand lens, the areoles and hook spines on a mammillaria. I know it's sad, but there we are.

6

THE KITCHEN GARDEN

The Spectator
February 2008

I have waited several years for this moment – in fact, ever since the late 1990s upsurge in interest in gardening began to fade, the press stopped talking about it as the new sex and the *jeunesse dorée* turned their fickle gaze elsewhere. Now, as partygoers shade their hungover eyes from the glare of financial reality and householders look in horror at their sky-rocketing bills, the talk is all of letting the holiday home, missing out on the cruise, keeping the old car going for another year and . . . and . . . even growing some vegetables.

I am sorry that it has taken an economic downturn to turn some people back to the preoccupations of their parents, but you can see why this might give me a quiet satisfaction. For I have always believed that a growing acquaintance with the soil and its fruits has a beneficent effect, even on the most urbane of boulevardiers. Moreover, too many people, put off by the cloth cap and tannin-stained-mug image of vegetable gardening, have no idea that it is a great deal more fun – and easier – than it used to be. Both techniques and the vegetables themselves have improved markedly in recent years.

There was a time when kitchen gardening, whether pursued on the allotment or in the garden, was ridiculously space-consuming. Vegetables were grown in wide apart, hoe-able rows, with gaps at intervals for the gardener to wheel a wheelbarrow along. These vegetables themselves were leafy, coarse and often pretty dull, particularly the old staples like potatoes, leeks, parsnips, celery and runner beans. The digging of the necessary trenches could only ever appeal to moles. But all that was before the benefits of the 'raised bed' and 'no-dig' systems were widely understood, and before there was a rich variety of vegetable cultivars that suited the private gardener as much, if not more, than the commercial grower.

A raised bed, if you have never seen one, is a 4-foot / 1.25-metre-wide rectangle, bounded by pressure-treated wooden boards and standing about 6 inches / 15 centimetres proud of the ground. It contains a fertile, well-drained mixture of soil and organic matter. In this mix, seed can be sown at roughly two-thirds the intervals necessary in conventional plots, both because of the soil's fertility and because the bed can be tended from narrow paths on both sides, so there is no harmful compaction of the growing medium itself. Small seed can be broadcast rather than sown in rows. Yields tend to be higher, weeding is a doddle and physical protection against pests and frost is much easier in these regular and confined spaces. Most importantly, exhausting autumn digging need only be done once; after that, keeping the soil aerated and fertile is simply a matter of an annual forking-in of organic matter, such as compost, rotted farmyard manure, wool shoddy, mushroom compost or whatever is locally available.

The plant breeders have come to our aid as well, in particular by producing vegetable varieties that are resistant to many pests and diseases. After all, no one is inclined to spray pesticides on to the food they eat. The carrot 'Flyaway' is genuinely left untouched by carrot fly, and there are now blight-resistant potatoes of Hungarian origin, called 'Sarpo Mira' and 'Sarpo Axona'.

Moreover, there are increasing numbers of vegetable cultivars, which can, and should, be eaten when young, and so suit the changes which there have been in our eating habits. 'Stereo' broad beans have pods tender enough to eat, while mange-tout 'Delikata' produces edible peas, as well as pods. The dwarf, bushy runner bean 'Hestia' does not need support, scallopini squashes are small enough for one person to eat and 'mesclun' mixes give as much variety as supermarket bags of salad leaves. Even the lack of a garden is no bar to vegetable growing now, since there are now so many 'compact' varieties, which can be grown in large pots or window boxes. If you don't want to be bothered with growing frost-tender vegetables (tomatoes, chilli peppers, aubergines) from seed, the mail-order seed merchants will send you young plants in spring; even hardy leeks, lettuces and brassicas can be bought this way.

What is more, some vegetables are sufficiently decorative to find a place in flower borders, thus confusing insect pests and giving the vegetables the benefit of fresh soil. There is, for example, Swiss chard 'Bright Lights', with its ribs striped red and yellow, and there are purple-skinned French beans and golden vegetables in plenty: tomato 'Sungold', courgette 'Goldrush', beetroot 'Golden Detroit', sweet pepper 'Golden Californian Wonder' and climbing French bean 'Neckar Gold'.

This talk of gold reminds me that 'We are stardust, we are golden, and we got to get ourselves back to the garden.' Quite right, Joni: so we have. And not just because there is nothing else we can afford to do at the moment.

The Spectator
April 2003

Years ago, as they say round here, there was such a thing as a 'blackthorn winter', a spell of harsh weather in late March and early April when the blackthorn flowers were white in the hedgerows. This year, there has been a 'blackthorn summer', almost three weeks of sunny, warm weather, after early morning mists and frosts. I don't think I can remember better weather in March, even in the year of the great drought, 1976. In that year, the weather was also windy, but in the last couple of weeks it has mainly been remarkably still. Moreover, the cold nights have meant, in this part of the east Midlands at least, that growth has not been helter-skelter; it is decorous and encompassable, not terrifying in its dynamic. Things are not yet getting out of hand.

Nevertheless, being conscious that a March dust is worth a king's ransom (as they don't say round here), a week last Sunday I abandoned, with facile and shaming casuistry, any plan to go to church, and went out to the vegetable garden instead. It was time to sow the peas.

I don't know if you have ever sowed peas. The job needs a sunny, birdsong morning and a well-cultivated soil to make it pleasant, for it is very fiddly, almost tiresome. Instead of simply being able to lay a taut line across the bed, draw out a shallow drill with an onion hoe along the line and sprinkle seed along that drill, as is usually the case with vegetables, it requires the making of a flat-bottomed drill, some 6 inches/15 centimetres wide and 1½ inches/3 centimetres deep.

The reason for this is simple. A single row of pea plants does not yield many peas for the effort, so it is necessary to sow densely, in a close zigzag, and support the resulting thickish herbage with sticks and string as it grows. A sharp, narrow spade must be pushed alongside the taut line to make this drill, and it is surprisingly tricky to make the drill both flat and of an equal depth. Once that is achieved, however, matters improve, for pea seed is large, hard and easy to place in three rows in the drill. After sowing, the soil must be carefully drawn back over with a rake, so that the seed is not dislodged, and tamped down with the rake head. Finally, a thick network of hazel twigs or a rectangle of chicken wire has to be laid on top to hinder birds and the infuriating activities of other people's cats, for whom a well-raked soil is an irresistible invitation. Some people stretch a network of black cotton across the rows between short stakes, but not only is this almost unendurably fiddly, but it must be an unpleasant sensation for birds who land on it, since the cotton is invisible to them.

Describing this workaday activity in such detail underlines for me an important point about gardening. With so much modern emphasis on the importance of good garden design, plant associations and all that stuff, it is easy to ignore the fact that there is often as much satisfaction to be had in some trivial task as in a grand scheme. And as much pleasure in an annual miniature miracle, like the leaves of a perennial pushing through the soil, as there is in viewing the Big Picture. A sunny March day finds me marvelling at the scent of primroses or tazetta narcissi, the claret-red young leaves of peonies, the furry buds of apple trees, the honey-bees, golden with pollen, in the crocuses. No pleasure in a well laid-out, generously planted July border is greater than that, since it lacks that vital spring ingredient, promise.

In any event, the Big Picture is a little blurred just now: beds of perennials still look quite bare and certainly flat, the tulips are all leaf, the biennials are not out, weeds are growing faster than cultivated plants, trees are yet to come into leaf, lawns are yellow and rank. Work done in March helps bring the Big Picture into focus. On that first Sunday morning of the second Gulf War, I could find welcome distraction from another Big Picture in complicated little tasks, and be grateful for the concentration that they required. And try not to feel obscurely badly about the chance to be out on a beautiful morning sowing peas in perfect peace.

The Spectator
March 2004

The future for the potato seems brighter this month than last, since the opening of the film *Sex Lives of the Potato Men*. This is an account, apparently (for I have not yet seen it), of the degraded lives of four vacuous and foul-mouthed young men who deliver potatoes to chip shops in Walsall. One critic asked whether this was the worst British comedy ever made, so I am as impatient as everyone else to see it. To be frank, I am less interested in the sex lives of the men than the portrayal of the potato. For the truth is that the reputation of the potato, among discerning gardeners at least, is presently high – and rising.

The potato has benefited lately from the benign collision of a number of modern facts of life: money, leisure, foodieness, deep-seated restlessness and sentimental nostalgia. Time was when gardeners grew only a limited range of reliable, heavy-cropping cultivars – 'Arran Pilot', 'Sharpe's Express', 'King Edward' and 'Majestic' – because they needed to. Now gardeners grow potatoes like 'Pink Fir Apple' and 'Catriona' because they are handsome or full of flavour, and the fact that the yields are lower no longer matters. A number of very old 'heirloom' or 'heritage' varieties, especially those with coloured skin and/or flesh, have been rescued from long-time obscurity; while worthy post-war cultivars have been pushed back into the limelight.

Several impressive displays of potato varieties have been staged in recent years at the Chelsea Flower Show and elsewhere, with upwards of two hundred different kinds on show. Heritage potatoes, as with heritage anything, attract enthusiasts: the present Potato King is a Scotsman called Alan Romans, who advises at least two seed companies. (Potato enthusiasts are often Scotsmen, by the by, since Scotland is where 'seed' potatoes are mostly grown, since, even now, colder winters mean that the dreaded peach-potato aphid, a vector for potato viruses, does not thrive north of the Border.)

What has happened to the potato has happened to several other vegetables as well, in particular tomatoes, although generally potatoes are more worthy of rescue than old tomato varieties in my experience. Hanging on to old cultivars, even if not in themselves much cop, is self-evidently worthwhile, if a large gene pool is to be maintained. Demand from amateur gardeners means that seed firms can justify continuing to offer unusual varieties, while Waitrose has done its bit to stimulate general demand.

Naturally, life being what it is, there is a tide flowing the other way. Under EU law, it is not possible to sell potato varieties to the public as seed unless they are on the National List or in the EU Common Catalogue, and the cost of maintaining the rarest heirloom potatoes for this list is prohibitive for small growers. However, thanks to an ingenious laboratory technique called micropropagation, it is possible to propagate the very rare varieties and sell them as guaranteed disease-free 'microplants' to enthusiasts. The market is tiny, but symbolically important.

One should not forget, however, that there are a great number of excellent varieties of potatoes, which were introduced after the last war, that have better yields and disease resistance than heirloom potatoes and often more taste than the very newest varieties. These have all the virtues one could want as a private gardener: the coveted coloured flesh, high dry matter (therefore usually full of flavour) and, most importantly, good resistance to potato cyst eelworms, blight, common scab and blackleg. So, in those years when I flinch from sentiment, as a great-aunt flinches from a draught, I plump for 'Red Duke of York' (1940s – first early), 'Charlotte' (1981 – second early), 'Nicola' (1973 – early maincrop) and 'Cara' (1976 – late maincrop).

Just occasionally, however, the romance of the potato enters my soul, and taste seems to matter more than yield, disease resistance or ease of peeling or cooking. In those seasons I am tempted by 'Arran Pilot' (1930 – first early), 'Edzell Blue' (late Victorian – second early), 'Belle de Fontenay' (1855 – early maincrop) and 'Arran Victory' (1918 – late maincrop).

The question of taste is usually a vexed one, since there is such a large element of subjectivity in it. In 1998, the Royal Horticultural Society carried out a trial of 'early' and 'second early' potatoes, that is the ones the public call 'new', and there was a distinct lack of unanimity amongst the judges as to which tasted the best. Finally, 'Charlotte' got the nod, with 'Winston' coming in as heaviest and largest cropper, a useful asset in a potato if you have only a small vegetable garden, but not always consistent with flavour, since large potatoes tend to have a high water content.

In case you are wondering, the commercial honours, especially for chipping, go to 'Maris Piper', a potato available at a supermarket near you. Introduced in 1964, it is resistant to eelworm, has shallow eyes, which make it easy to peel, and has a high dry matter content. It is, however, irresistible to slugs and falls prey to scab. So a fitting potato for those lads in Walsall, then.

The Spectator
July 2006

I have driven through the village of Aynho in south Northamptonshire several times lately and, each time, I have been heartened by the number of young apricot trees that are growing against the walls of the cottages in the main street. For, in recent years, I had become a little anxious that a long village tradition was coming gradually to an end. But it seems not. Perhaps it was the result of a Millennium initiative by the parish council to provide each villager with an apricot plant, or even a working-out of the collective consciousness.

In any event, it is cheering to see them, for apricots have always grown particularly well in Aynho – so much so that it is still known as the Apricot Village. An erstwhile head gardener at the big house, Aynhoe Park, Ted Humphris (in a memoir he wrote about working there for fifty years, published in 1969), recounted how apricots had been grown against the walls of stone village houses facing south and west 'since feudal times'. He said they particularly enjoyed the stony, sandy, limey marl, which is the soil there, and received all the water they required because the houses were without gutters. Sufficient water at the root prevents the cracking of the fruits as they swell and it also seems to make die-back less likely. Moreover, the apricot flowers early, in March, so it was a great advantage that Aynho stands on a south-west slope, and frost drains quickly downhill. All that is still true, apart from the fact that the houses have gutters, and the roads are macadamized. The apricot grown was either 'Breda', he thought, or 'Moor Park', and when a villager's tree died, it would be replaced by a 'Moor Park' grown on in the gardens of Aynhoe Park.

If it were indeed 'Moor Park', it would not have been grown there 'since feudal times', of course, as the first references to it in fruit catalogues are in the 1780s. I have a particular affection for it, and grow it in my garden, for two reasons which have nothing horticultural about them. Firstly, because my grandmother spent much of her youth at a house called Moor Park in Hertfordshire. This Palladian mansion with a 'Capability' Brown landscaped park was owned by her grandfather until just after the First World War, when it became a golf club house. (This circumstance was relished by John Betjeman, keen golfer as well as architectural historian, in his poem 'Metroland'.) Secondly, a 'Moor Park' apricot is mentioned by the miserly Mrs Norris in *Mansfield Park* as having cost 'seven shillings'. The exchange between Mrs Norris and Dr Grant concerning this apricot is Jane Austen at her most sprightly. I was given mine as a present by my brothers, so I wouldn't dream of asking them how much it cost.

The apricot is the lazy man's peach, really, since it likes the same situation, yet is not bedevilled by peach leaf curl, a disease which requires that peach trees be protected from damp in winter to prevent the fungal spores from germinating on the unfolding leaf buds. Moreover, although on walls you grow apricots as fans, you prune them as you would a plum rather than a peach, and that is an easier regime to learn. Early flowering means hand pollinating and fleece protection against frost, but that is no more than you must do for peaches anyway.

'Moor Park' or, as the catalogues have it 'Moorpark', produces large, fat, orange-yellow fruits at the end of August, if you grow it against a warm wall, which really you have to. There is also a clone of it, called 'Early Moorpark', which fruits a fortnight earlier and is thus the obvious choice for those who live north of the Trent. Though I say 'obvious choice', others may dispute that, because it has a tendency to bear biennially and is prone to canker die-back. Mine is as miserly as Mrs Norris: this year we are looking forward to eating one fruit (provided it doesn't drop off in the drought). These days, the wiseacres will tell you to grow the modern cultivars 'Tomcot' or 'Flavourcot'. 'Flavourcot' is said to be hardier than the 'Victoria' plum, so can be grown in the open in the south of England.

Some say Sir William Temple (1628–99), the garden-minded diplomat and writer who so admired the earlier Jacobean house at Moor Park that he named his own seat in Surrey after it, imported the 'Moor Park' apricot originally from Brussels, while others lean to the view that Admiral Lord Anson brought it home to the Hertfordshire Moor Park, where he lived until his death in 1762. It must be plain which version I favour, although you need not depend on that. All I know for certain is that my 'Moor Park' is a solid joy and lasting treasure, lovely in flower and always neat in leaf, with bronze-coloured new growths, and I really couldn't care less if I don't get fruit from it every year. I have a feeling that the people of Aynho might well agree.

The Spectator
January 2006

When I was a very young gardener, few things made me more impatient than the conservatism of older ones. Conservatism seemed to be calcified in the very bones of the old boys I worked with, who appeared almost ridiculous to me in their subfusc trousers held up by leather belts, their waistcoats, their flat caps and their pipes of tobacco. They seemed to want to look and sound as much like Edwardian head gardeners as they could (these having been their boyhood heroes, I suppose) and their ideas, though often rather charming, were scarcely more advanced. They had practical skills that we can only dream of now, although, in retrospect, I see they were not invariably right. I remember, for example, being taught to pot up pelargoniums by ramming the loam-based potting compost round the roots hard with a wooden stick. How these men imagined that any pot plant could thrive when its roots were deliberately starved of oxygen is beyond me.

Now I am rather older, I find conservatism creeps on, like a low river mist, threatening to obscure interesting new ideas. I have to fight the tendency. I catch myself tut-tutting at the sloppy gardening methods exhibited on *Gardeners' World*, as if it really mattered. The truth is that gardening has changed in many ways and – if one wants to be neutral and objective about these things – it had to.

One aspect of contemporary gardening I have had difficulty in the past accepting is the vastly increased use of dwarfing rootstocks for fruit trees, which are sold for garden planting. (The scion, or variety, of a tree is grafted on to a rootstock, which controls its vigour.) There are a number of dwarfing, semi-dwarfing and semi-vigorous rootstocks; in the case of apples, they are distinguished from each other by M or MM numbers, while pear rootstocks are called Quince 'A' (semi-vigorous) and Quince 'C' (semi-dwarfing).

These dwarfing and semi-dwarfing rootstocks are fine, indeed necessary, for commercial orchards, since they come into 'bearing' quickly and they are short enough to be sprayed, pruned and picked from the ground. The soil has to be fertile for them, and the most dwarfing stocks need to be staked, for they are weak, but that is not normally a problem. However, in gardens, these neat and tidy trees seem dull and jejune to me, only really justified if the trees are to be trained in 'restricted' forms, that is as 'step-overs', espaliers, cordons or fans. The beauty of a tall, crooked and eccentric standard tree on an M25 rootstock cannot be easily exaggerated, nor its contribution to atmosphere, in a cottage garden especially.

Cherries, however, are another matter, as I hope I am just about to find out. I have ordered for January delivery three young trees grafted on to 'Gisela 5' or 'G5', a newish rootstock which has a more dwarfing effect than the longer-established 'Colt'. This rootstock restricts the height of a cherry to 6 to 8 feet/1.75 to 2.5 metres tall. The beauty of it is that I shall be able to plant these three trees inside my fruit cage. They will take the place of strawberries, recently removed after virus had begun to undermine their energy and fruitfulness.

The main reason I wish to plant these trees in the fruit cage is because cherries are the very food of the gods to blackbirds and other common garden avians. Netting a cherry grown in the open is never wholly successful and is often simply a disagreeable way of trapping birds. Pretty as the white cherry blossom undoubtedly is (or it would not have had a shoe polish named after it, surely?), it is not a good enough reason to grow sweet cherries. Cherries are also by far the best if picked when ripe, which they are not for shop sale, and they keep for only a few days. That is why you really have to grow them yourself.

The exact choice of varieties has been governed by a mix of epicureanism and practicality, in about equal measure. 'Stella' and 'Sunburst' are self-fertile and healthy varieties, the first with large red juicy fruits, the second with black ones, while 'Merton Glory' is a self-sterile variety, which happens to be pollinated by 'Stella' and 'Sunburst', and is a 'white' cherry. It is not, strictly speaking, white, but has a yellow skin, which is flushed crimson, and white juice. It is a good pollinator of other varieties. All three are ready to pick in July.

The growing of exotic fruit, such as cherries, used to be the preserve (ouch) of those employed gardeners I once worked with, who were the only people with the time and patience to cultivate them properly. Now it seems any gardener can grow them. Even when at my most conservative, I can hardly regret that.

'Borderlines', *Daily Telegraph*
27 October 2007

'If you knew then what you know now, would you still have planted an Asian pear?' asked my husband recently. As penetrating questions go, it was a good one, for the Asian (Nashi) pear 'Shinseiki', which I grow in my small orchard, has masses of round, yellow, attractive fruit, which beckon you from across the garden, but they are gritty in texture, watery rather than juicy and absolutely not in the same stratosphere of taste sensation as a 'Comice' or even a 'Beth'. Yet in September and early October, we were picking them by the bucketload, and dutifully eating them each evening in order that not one should go to waste. (Not only are they gritty and watery but, being early maturing, they don't keep well.) We used to enjoy them when we had only a few, but now we feel as if we are drowning in them.

These pears point up a dilemma which all garden fruit growers have to grapple with sooner, or rather later. When you first plant top or soft fruit, the first few years are years of relative famine. In fact, the first year you get nothing at all, because all the books tell you to take off the flowers to allow the plant to establish itself vegetatively first. The second year, you find yourself carefully picking the one apple that ripens and ceremoniously carving it up for everyone in the family to enjoy a taste. You are impatient for more. The next year, you have ten apples and life seems very good indeed. The year after that you have bushels of them and suddenly you find you can't give them away.

That is when your life begins to change. You no longer take a holiday in September, because there are the crab apples to make into jelly and the damsons into jam, while October is out because you have the pears and quinces to pick and store, and the apples to crush and juice. Even weekend lunch invitations get in the way of so much happy, productive activity. Should you somehow find time to entertain, your guests can expect pork and apple casserole, followed by pear tart or autumn raspberry mousse.

Your kitchen surfaces and fridge salad drawers become cluttered with odd windfall apples and pears, of diverse variety, which you have picked up and brought inside so they 'don't go to waste'. In my case, they sometimes get forgotten and sit on the side, gradually developing pustules of brown rot, which finally galvanizes me into throwing them away.

Actually, I wouldn't have it any other way. I do believe that the best garden moment for me this summer came when my globe-trotting son told me that my 'Moor Park' apricots tasted better than the ones he had eaten in Syria. And I am conscious that I should never take Nature's bounty for granted, but enjoy it while I may.

So, what to do with those tasteless Asian pears? Well, I could get out the fruit press and make some pear juice, or even perry, I guess, but what is wrong with leaving the sound ones on the ground for birds, butterflies and small mammals to eat? After all, they need sustenance as much as I do, yet are rather less fussy about the taste.

The Spectator
September 2006

There are, as we all know, many disadvantages to going away on holiday, not least the fact – so ably nailed by Alain de Botton – that we are forced to take ourselves with us. How relaxing it would be to leave home without one's own deficiencies and inability to enjoy oneself when doing nothing. By the same token, some absolute essentials for happiness have to be left at home: in my case, my dessert plum trees.

This year, in mid-August, we went away for just one week. The 'Denniston's Superb' greengages were just ripening when we left, so I picked as many as I could to put in the fridge. I topped up the sugar solution in the wasp traps hanging from the branches. A week later, we returned to find that almost all had been substantially damaged by wasps (the traps having dried up in the meantime), while the rest had fallen to the ground. Those picked for the fridge were beyond all human expression delicious, but there were not nearly enough of them to satisfy our craving for this sweet, juicy-fleshed, round, greenish-yellow dessert plum.

The plum (*Prunus domestica*) is a hybrid developed from at least two wild *Prunus* species; it arose many centuries ago, probably in the Caucasus, and was then carried westwards by merchants and other travellers. Plum stones have been found at Roman archaeological sites in this country. These days, there are upwards of a hundred varieties. Plums have skins varying in colour from yellow and pink to deep purple; they can be dessert, that is, capable of being eaten off the tree, culinary or 'dual-purpose'. Greengages, which are botanically closely related, but distinctive in appearance, are green or yellow, smaller and more rounded than other plums. The greengage is named after Sir Thomas Gage, an amateur botanist and entomologist of Hengrave Hall, Suffolk, whose brother, a Roman Catholic priest, sent trees back from France, where it has always been known as 'Reine-Claude', early in the eighteenth century. The gardener lost the label so it came to be known, and disseminated, as 'Green Gage'.

Plums, of whatever kind, will never be as popular with gardeners as apples and pears for reasons which are not far to seek, but mildly dispiriting, nevertheless. Wasps, bacterial canker, the fungal disease silver leaf, the shortness of their season, the necessity of thinning the young fruits and their vulnerability to frost, since they flower in March, all tell against them in the public mind. But where crop size is not very important, as is the case for most gardeners, and where simple precautions (such as pruning only on a dry day in spring or summer) are perfectly possible, it seems almost perverse to ignore them. They can also be trained in a fan shape on south or west-facing walls, which saves space and makes frost damage much less likely.

The only immutable rule with plums is to remember to thin them in June, to

2 inches/5 centimetres apart, so that the remaining fruits develop maximum flavour, the branches do not break under the weight of fruit in a good year and they do not resort to biennial bearing – that is, producing fruit only every two years. Garden owners look at me as if I and my trolley have finally parted company when I mention thinning, as if it were something that only glassy-eyed fanatics would bother with. But what is more pleasant on an early June day than picking off small, immature plum fruits in the sunshine? It beats weeding any day.

If, by chance, you are thinking of planting a fruit tree, or two, in your garden this autumn, spare a thought for dessert plums. Then spare another for the best and most suitable varieties: ignore the dual-purpose 'Victoria', however reliable, since you can buy it in any supermarket and its taste is only so-so. Plump instead for ones that are harder to find but much sweeter, such as 'Jubilaeum' or 'Avalon'. The blue-skinned 'Opal' ripens in late July, while you could still be picking the delectable, dark-fleshed, pruney 'Angelina Burdett' in early September. As for greengages, I suggest 'Early Transparent Gage', 'Denniston's Superb' or 'Cambridge Gage'. And, if you need a respectable excuse for avoiding an August or early September holiday, then the harvesting of dessert plums will provide you with one. After this year's domestic debacle, I have high hopes of being allowed, even encouraged, to stay at home next summer.

The Spectator
October 2003

Next Tuesday is Apple Day and somewhere near you this weekend there will be an apple-centred event, offering tastings, expert advice and identification of garden varieties, children's games and a lot else. Of this I have no doubt. Founded by the charity Common Ground in 1990 to highlight the rapid loss of orchards in this country as well as the loss of our regional apple heritage, Apple Day is an annual piproaring success in city, town and country. Apple varieties which no one had ever heard of have become almost commonplace, for the gardening media has taken up the cause with alacrity, extolling the virtues of 'Laxton's Epicure', 'Ross Nonpareil', 'Pitmaston Pine Apple', 'Devonshire Quarrenden', 'Cornish Gilliflower' and many other quaintly named varieties with equally quaint histories.

I yield to no one in my admiration for the work of Common Ground in championing the cause of local distinctiveness, of which the apple is a potent symbol, for Brogdale Horticultural Trust in encouraging the public enjoyment of home-grown fruit and for the few specialist nurseries like Keeper's Nursery in Kent who continued to propagate some of the older and trickier cultivars at a time when no one was asking for them. However, there is now a danger of heritage apple snobbery, especially amongst some of my colleagues. Autumnal articles on apples often declare the superiority of old varieties, and feature modern sorts only rarely.

Sure, I grow a number of venerable varieties, in particular 'Barnack Beauty' and 'Lord Burghley' (introduced 1870 and 1834 respectively), which were both raised within a few miles of my garden. Although 'Barnack Beauty' is a good apple, keeping well, and with an excellent colour, 'Lord Burghley' is a washout and only sentiment keeps it in the orchard, for the crop is indifferent and the growth unthrifty and disease prone. I also grow the russet 'Ashmead's Kernel' (1700), often recommended, but which does not crop well for me, being prone to a mineral deficiency called bitter pit. Indeed, since we have bee hives and I don't want to spray with pesticides, at least some of the apple varieties in my orchard have been chosen for disease resistance and have been raised in the last eighty years. For example, I favour 'Sunset' (1933), which is the variety for all those 'Cox's Orange Pippin' lovers who know what a difficult apple it is to grow successfully. I picked one off the ground yesterday and it was delicious.

I have space in my garden to experiment, and am grateful that I can grow both old and new. The problem with great emphasis on ancient varieties with charming names, however, is that it is not a lot of help if you live in a new house with a small garden, on the outskirts of Oxford, say. In these circumstances, you might well be tempted by what you read to plant 'Blenheim Orange', which arose in Woodstock about 1740, and is a late-maturing apple which can be used for both dessert and culinary purposes. It sounds ideal, initially, especially as it is a very pretty apple, and has local connections and a picturesque name. However, were you to enquire further, you would discover that it is triploid – that is, it needs two other types of apple to pollinate it well and is not a good pollinator of other apple varieties; it is partially tip-bearing, which means it is not straightforward to prune; it is biennial bearing (that is, it only produces a good crop every other year) and it is prone to scab disease. Since there are likely to be few other apple trees in the neighbouring new gardens, you would be better advised to plant one of the recently bred, self-fertile, disease-resistant and frost-hardy varieties like 'Red Falstaff', 'Red Devil' or 'Scrumptious'. 'Red Falstaff' is hugely prolific, with lovely blossom in spring and, if picked late (in mid-October), will keep until next spring, while 'Red Devil' develops the colour of a cricket ball, and has pink flesh, a crisp taste suggesting strawberries and really excellent disease resistance. 'Scrumptious' has a rich, sweet yet crisp flavour and a thin skin, and can be eaten off the tree any time in September.

Of course, the name 'Scrumptious', though descriptive of the taste, is hardly likely to appeal to the 'Pitmaston Pine Apple' tendency. As a nurseryman friend said about a cultivar called 'Prima', which he could never persuade people to buy, despite its obvious qualities: 'I would have sold far more if I had renamed it 'Lady Lucy's Pearmain'.' But the truth is that, if you only have room in your garden for one tree, and you want an apple that produces generous quantities of clean, delicious fruit without a lot of messing about, 'Scrumptious' is the one. Although you may search in vain for a mention of it in this weekend's papers.

'Borderlines', *Daily Telegraph*
15 October 2005

It is not often openly admitted (although we all tacitly accept the fact) that gardening is character-forming. And we don't mean that as a compliment. Most of us would far rather hang on to the characters we had before, thank you very much, and are not at all keen to have them formed further. In theory, perhaps; in practice, definitely not.

There are a number of gardening activities, however, that test our mettle and character to the utmost. Scarifying a large lawn with a springbok rake, for example, is one of those, as is spraying nettles with Roundup. Strimming long grass on a hot day comes into this category, as does weeding in a cold, thin drizzle.

It is just as well, therefore, that there are so many tasks which are genuinely balm for the soul, or I for one would give the whole thing up as a bad job. Picking sweet peas for the house on a summer's evening must be close to the top of my list, along with sowing seeds in spring, pruning espalier pear trees and picking summer raspberries.

It is not just physical aspects of gardening which can test us, however, and this has been much on my mind lately as I gather what passes – ha! – for a fruit crop this year. When we first take up gardening our optimism spills over like fizzy Coca-Cola; we cannot believe that there can be such thing as failure, or disappointment. Everything we plant comes up, everything we sow germinates, and it all seems a breeze. But the more experienced we become, the more we fear, even expect, disappointment, and nowhere is this truer than in the matter of fruit growing. For with fruit, there are a number of factors almost entirely outside our control.

The fruit gardener, by the expense of effort and money, can minimize the likelihood of failure but never completely eradicate it. We can build walls, plant shelter belts, keep bees, encourage solitary insects as much as we like but weather conditions such as we 'enjoyed' this last spring can still do for us in the end. Certainly, this year, in this garden, what plum blossom escaped being actually frosted was cruelly withered by cold winds and cold nights, despite a sheltering hornbeam hedge and willow belt. The crop count sounds like the classified football results: Oullins Gage 2; Victoria Plum 5. Damsons 6, Old Green Gage 0. The matches between Peach 'Peregrine' and Apricot 'Moor Park', and Quinces 'Vranja' and 'Meech's Prolific', were abandoned.

I do try to be philosophical, and accept that some years the garden works less well than in others; and to be grateful for the fruit that really is reliable, if ever so slightly dull: like blackcurrants, rhubarb, autumn raspberries and 'Newton Wonder' apples. I try not to hanker after those fruits which are not weatherproof, simply savouring them in the seasons when the weather does not confound them. After all, one of the reasons I am a gardener is that, despite all the evidence to the contrary, I retain an unshakeable belief that next year is bound to be better.

7

'Borderlines', *Daily Telegraph*
7 October 2006

I measure out my life, not in coffee spoons like J. Alfred Prufrock, but in judging engagements at village flower shows. Every summer for the past twenty-two years, these shows have been part of a stately, unchanging, rather comforting ritual. When I wake on August Bank Holiday Monday, my first thought is: 'Ah, this morning, I am at Nassington.' No doubt, many other amateur judges map out their time in the same way, since we are the (more-or-less) willing slaves of the iron determination and beady eye of a thousand flower show secretaries.

All these years I have judged flowers, fruit and vegetables in tandem with one man, who kindly and patiently taught me the craft. In 1984, Nicholas was head gardener on a big estate. Now his expertise is required in the planteria of a large independent garden centre and he writes and broadcasts locally as well. He is our county's greatest gardening expert. In 1984, I was very much the judicial apprentice; now, however, I like to think we are equals. Well almost. Sometimes, we disagree, but we never fall out. We try to be humane; disqualifying 'Not as schedule' exhibits pains us dreadfully. Most exhibitors don't cheat, but they also don't count very carefully, either. If the schedule calls for twelve raspberries and there are thirteen on a plate, we eat one. If there are only eleven, we are stuck.

I don't know how other judges approach the task, but we talk incessantly while we work. We mostly discuss the exhibits in front of us, but we also catch up on the gossip, and comment on the season and weather. However, on the Saturday of the Bank Holiday weekend this year, at Wansford, even our chatter came to an abrupt halt. We were standing in front of a white-clothed trestle table, on which were placed the Collection of Fruits exhibits, consisting of four entries. Our jaws definitely dropped.

Each exhibit, laid out on a large plate or tray, consisted of five or six types of fruit: peaches, grapes, damsons, crab apples, raspberries, plums and figs for the most part, this being late August. The reason for the stupefied silence was the exceptional quality of the fruit displayed. (Fruit, generally, is the Cinderella at village shows.) Moreover, each exhibitor had taken care to retain the bloom on the plums, to pick the peaches without bruising, to keep the stalks on the crab apples, in short to show everything to its best advantage. One or two had even thinned the grapes carefully with scissors at some point, so that the bunches were as uniform and inviting as in a Dutch still life. We had the deuce of a job deciding which should come first, and we even added a Highly Commended for the unplaced exhibit, something we never normally do, except in the children's classes, *pour encourager.*

I searched my memory in vain for another year so good for fruit, the result of a late spring, when even plum blossom escaped the frosts, the rain in May and hot weather in late June and July. In a season which was extremely trying to vegetable gardeners (there were plenty of limp lettuces and cankered parsnips about the shows this summer) fruit growers seem to have had an *annus mirabilis.* I hope a lot of gardeners saw that fruit, and took note – and heart.

'Borderlines', *Daily Telegraph*
31 July 2004

I blame it on my school and its marked achievement ethic. If I had been given a prize, any prize, even the Effort Cup, the summer I left, I might never have battled all my adult life with an unquenchable competitiveness. Amongst many other things, this spurs me to enter exhibits at our village flower show, held on a Saturday in mid-July.

In 2003, I won the cut-glass rose bowl for 'the most points in the Fruit Section', fruit being very dear to my heart and the timing of the show coinciding nicely with the soft fruit season. Early on this year, I caught myself resolving that I would try to win it again. So, despite a commitment to help judge at our local town flower show at ten-thirty, two hours earlier I was to be found in the village hall, laying out a variety of horticultural exhibits, particularly soft fruit. With me was Cynthia, who works alongside me in the garden on Tuesdays, and who had volunteered to help, for I am afraid I have rather infected her with this competitiveness. Certainly, our conversations for weeks before had revolved around whether the peas would be over, the rhubarb too coarse, the potatoes too scabby, the white currants too sparse, to 'enter'.

Our most agonizing decision that morning had been whether to sacrifice three fruits from the fan-trained peach tree, to accompany the raspberries and gooseberries in the 'Three kinds of fruit' class, or trust to the loganberries instead. In the end, the peaches won our vote for, though not yet quite ripe, they were without blemish, already deliciously red on one side and as downy as a teenager's chin. We felt a sharp pang of regret as we removed them from the tree, but it seemed to be in a good cause.

The exhibiting finished, I went off to discharge my judicial obligations, with my husband's words 'Judge not, that ye be not judged' ringing in my ears. Ha, ha, very funny. You probably think that judges are bound to make good exhibitors, but that is far from being automatically the case. After all, between the idea and the reality, between the motion and the act, falls the Shadow. Just because I know what judges are looking for does not mean I can produce it – or better than other people, at least. I suppose the reason why I am drawn to exhibiting is because it proves my mettle as a gardener. It is all very well bossily telling other people what to do, but should one not test one's right to do that every so often?

Successful exhibitors have a number of common characteristics: experience (the more years under your belt the better), single-mindedness and the capacity, and desire, to put in the hours. It is hard work and attention to detail, not diplomas or money, which produce good exhibits. Flower shows are as nakedly democratic as it gets, which is partly why they are so precious.

In the end, the day turned out disastrously for me. Although my stuff had not come first in every class I entered, it had done well enough to win me both the cut-glass bowl for Fruit and the silver cup for the most points in the Horticultural Section. That wasn't testing my mettle, that was showing off, big-time. No wonder I was rather pink as I collected my prizes. But, if my friends and neighbours thought it arrogance and unworthy pride (and who could blame them if they did?), they were kind enough not to tell me so. Perhaps they were silently resolving to beat me next year. I do hope so.

The Spectator
June 2005

This was my thirtieth consecutive visit to the Chelsea Flower Show. You may think that means I have become a little weary and difficult to impress: been there, seen that, got the glossy catalogue, tripped over the celebrities. But, as I walked around the Great Pavilion on Tuesday morning, amongst the most knowledgeable and avid gardening crowd in the world, I felt something strange in my chest, which felt like a warming of the heart.

This has been a bloody awful spring for gardeners. There has been too little rain, too many cold winds from the north and east, a few boiling hot days and, worst of all, late frosts. Exhibitor after exhibitor told me of their difficulties in timing the flowering of their plants for the last week in May. Many use polythene tunnels in which to grow their Chelsea stock yet complained that they were moving the stuff in and out all the time, so variable were the temperatures. The only mercy was that there had not been a heatwave the week before – as sometimes happens – which puts flowers past their best, just as they are being offloaded from the vans.

And yet, and yet. The quality of plants on show at Chelsea this year was as high, generally, as I have ever seen it. True, some plants were not yet flowering as they should early in the week but, considering that the flower show now lasts an extra day (the Royal Horticultural Society's response to calls over many years to cut the overcrowding), this was no bad thing. Generally, the exhibitors had managed to pull off the most difficult trick of all, and had done it with a dedication which simply beggars belief. Despite the fact that they cannot sell their plants (except at knockdown prices at the end of the show), nurserymen, large and small, go to extraordinary lengths, and a great deal of expense, to put on a display which lasts just five days.

Nor is this perfectionism and dedication confined to British exhibitors. There are a number of international stands at Chelsea, most notably Kirstenbosch Botanic Gardens from Cape Town which, like me, has been at the show every year since 1975. For three decades, through good times and bad, Kirstenbosch has demonstrated that the wonderful, vulnerable flora of the Cape deserves our admiration and attention and that there are people of the highest quality dedicating their lives to its understanding and protection.

Outside, amongst the show gardens, the Ecover Chelsea Pensioners' Garden, designed by Julian Dowle, not only won the hearts of the public but turned the heads of the judges, who gave it Best in Show. For 'A Soldier's Dream of Blighty', Dowle worked closely with Chelsea Pensioners, taking account of their memories and attitudes; he designed a garden in front of a thatched country pub, complete with pre-war vegetable cultivars, grown by the pensioners, as well as village green, pond and all. In Chelsea show garden design terms it was the oldest of old hat, but the finish was excellent, and the whole thing touching in its sincerity.

What warmed my heart most, however, because its undoubted humanitarian success is based on the immutable cold logic of chemistry and botany, was a scientific exhibit staged by Rothamsted Research (formerly the government-run Rothamsted Experimental Station in Hertfordshire) in the Lifelong Learning section; to the credit of the RHS, this is now in a prominent position in the Great Pavilion, rather than tucked away in a side tent where no one much could find it, as in past years.

Even so, most Chelsea visitors will have passed this stand by, I suspect, since it wasn't particularly colourful or alluring. They may perhaps have fleetingly wondered why an African woman, wrapped in a woolly cardigan against the treacherous spring cold, was standing answering questions.

She was Mary, a Kenyan smallholder, whose life and prospects have been transformed by Rothamsted's research. In East Africa, sorghum, maize and millet, staple crops for smallholders, are often devastated by a pretty but wicked and prolific plant called witchweed (*Striga*), which parasitizes cereal roots, and can cause complete destruction of the crop. These crops are also damaged by stem borer moths. Rothamsted Research, under the direction of Professor John Pickett, together with the International Centre of Insect Physiology and Ecology (no, I hadn't either), the Kenya Agricultural Institute and the Kenyan Ministry of Agriculture, have been funded by a number of charities, such as the Gatsby Foundation, to do work on 'companion planting'. The result has been the discovery that an African pea-relative called silver leaf desmodium, if planted between the rows of cereals, gives off an odour which repels stem borers while, at the same time, releasing chemicals from its roots which inhibit the witchweed. If Napier grass (*Pennisetum purpureum*) is planted round the shamba boundary, it lures highly susceptible stem borers away from the crop. This is a form of companion planting known as the 'push-pull' system.

Desmodium, being a legume, has the capacity to enrich the soil with nitrogen and, moreover, along with the Napier grass, it is fed by Mary to her cows.

Before embracing this system, she had one cow; now she has four. This is one practical, sober, unshowy way to help Make Poverty History. Heartwarming, or what?

'Borderlines', *Daily Telegraph*
9 June 2007

Peeling a grape, darning a sock, painting your toenails: there are some achievements in life which somehow don't quite justify the labour involved. Until this year, I was inclined to think that making a garden at the Chelsea Flower Show was another. Surely, however beautiful, interesting or innovative the result, it could not be worth the heroic efforts, nerve-jangling anxiety and dragging exhaustion that exhibitors wear proudly, like stripes on their back? Well, I was dead wrong. Now that I have helped to plan and plant one – 'The Transit of Venus Chic Garden' for my old college, New Hall, Cambridge* – I have changed my mind.

As garden makers will tell you, it is a long hard road to Chelsea. The process takes about eighteen months. First, your detailed application must be accepted by the Royal Horticultural Society, and many are received but few are chosen. With the exception of our garden designer, the excellent Sue Goss, none of our team had any experience of making a garden there and most of us were professional gardeners rather than seasoned landscape contractors. So all credit, as footballers say, to the RHS for giving us the opportunity.

Next there is the need to find sponsorship. New Hall is an educational institution for academically gifted young women and, although supportive in many ways, could not possibly bankroll the project. However, we used the college expertise in fund-raising, and all the money promised came from local firms, or from individuals – some of them 'old girls' – who just liked what we were trying to do. We also received help in kind, for example, the extraordinarily sticky Chelsea buns provided by the iconic Fitzbillies bakery in Cambridge, which revitalized us every time we hit a wall of tiredness, and the Jura limestone mulch provided by Specialist Aggregates of Stafford, a company owned by a past student.

My task was to plan, help source and plant the 'prismatic' or rainbow planting, which was both integral to the garden's concept and necessary if the garden was to be aesthetically pleasing. Like the other exhibitors, I fussed and fretted through what was a more than usually unpredictable spring. Would the Oriental poppies be past their best, would *Eremurus* 'Cleopatra' deign to flower? These thoughts kept me awake at night.

After spending four very long days planting, I found I looked at the other show gardens with a heightened perception, as if I had taken some mind-altering substance which allowed me to view them with a rather disconcerting intensity. So developed had my critical faculties temporarily become that I observed the way each pebble was placed, each water droplet dripped, each rose petal crimped where the hot sun had touched it.

Although back to normal now, I know that this year's show will live on as a bright jewel in my memory. This is partly because of the fun I had working in a highly motivated team and partly because of the enthusiasm of the knowledgeable crowds. Visitors were ranked five deep in front of the garden, as they strained to hear the Senior Tutor's brilliant explanation of parallax, to view the black dot of Venus against the 'sun' reflected in a mirror and to comment on the solar-yellow spires of *Verbascum* 'Gainsborough' and the shooting stars of *Allium schubertii*. Oh yes, it was worth it all right.

* *Recently renamed Murray Edwards College.*

The Spectator
June 2006

There was an unexpected outbreak of common sense at the Chelsea Flower Show this year. I looked hard for the usual silliness to laugh at, but I was hard pressed to find much. There was much sober purposefulness and little evident desire to *épater le bourgeois*. Most emperors had obviously decided that the weather warranted them wearing their oldest and warmest clothes. Was it the absence from the show of Diarmuid Gavin and his contrived spats, perhaps, or the fact that the show's sponsor was Saga Insurance for the first time, or did the chill breeze of current commercial reality wither any desire for wackiness? I cannot say. All I know was that it was so.

The show gardens were, almost without exception, exemplary. We all missed Christopher Bradley-Hole this year, but the other big double-barrelled gun, Tom Stuart-Smith, was on mid-season form for the *Daily Telegraph*, and carried off the best show garden prize with his clean-lined formal design, defined by high-quality silvered oak decking, ironstone sett paths and rusty-orange corten steel panels and tanks, all of which was subverted by dense drifts and clumps of purple, white and rusty-orange planting, and informal cloud box hedges. Even this magician could not make a silk purse out of *Viburnum rhytidophyllum*, but otherwise it was a triumph.

Designers are producing gardens which we might actually want to own. We can't afford them, of course, but at least they bear some relation to our aspirations. The small 'courtyard', chic' and 'city' gardens (mainly 13 by 16 feet/4 by 5 metres in size) are particularly interesting from this point of view. They have become a notable feature of Chelsea, introduced to attract young, inexperienced designers of talent with limited budgets (£5,000 to £25,000). The homage to Robin Spencer (creator of one of the finest twentieth-century gardens, York Gate, near Leeds, now in the care of the charity Perennial) by the garden design students of Leeds Metropolitan University, was especially good, with its rich, but controlled, mixture of local landscaping materials, such as make York Gate itself so memorable.

In the Great Pavilion, a particularly trying cold, dry, late spring, followed by a wet, windy May, scarcely caused the exhibitors to break stride. There were few gimmicks – except for the rather endearing Bournemouth Borough Council exhibit with its giant deckchair and figures sculpted out of sand – and the quality of the plants, despite the season, was exemplary. There were new Polish-bred clematis from Thorncroft Clematis Nursery, an enormous and well-displayed stand of perennials from the East Anglian branch of the Hardy Plant Society, and yet another brilliant display of roses from Peter Beales Roses. How easy it is to take excellence for granted! If, like me, you have clocked up more than thirty Chelseas, there is a tendency to treat as commonplace what is, in fact, exceptional.

The most blasé Chelsea visitor, however, could not take one stand for granted. This was the gold-medal-winning Writhlington School orchid project, in the Lifelong Learning section, usually a place of worthy and informative, but not always riveting, exhibits consisting of fungi or parasites or, sometimes, both at once.

Thanks to the energy and drive of one teacher, Simon Pugh-Jones, with support from the head teacher, Marie Getheridge, some 250 pupils from this rural comprehensive school south of Bath raise orchids from seed, sell them and use the money for partnership conservation projects and school expeditions in Guatemala, Costa Rica and Sikkim. Pupils are given an orchid genus to look after, and the enthusiasm and knowledge with which they talk about their charges would do credit to a Kew scientist (which several are aiming to become). These young people have learned a number of lessons – science, of course, but also global interdependency, teamwork and how to pass on knowledge. And, as the head teacher pointed out to me, the value of deferred gratification: one lad, Callum Swift, sowed the seed of the native terrestrial orchid *Dactylorrhiza fuchsii* after he arrived at the school, aged eleven. Now in the Lower Sixth, he has just seen it flower for the first time.

Yes, it was a very good Chelsea; for the 157,000 people who saw it over five days, at least. That is, however, only a very small percentage of the keen gardeners in this country. Everyone else is dependent on television coverage, which, as usual, let them down. Considering the advantages the BBC has over the print journalists, in being able to use a visual medium for a highly visual event, it yearly squanders the opportunity. The coverage, and there were eleven hours of it, seemed too often superficial, lacking conciseness and bite, and with camerawork which would unsettle a butterfly. They were only saved from complete embarrassment by the competence of Alan Titchmarsh, Joe Swift and Carol Klein, the latter mostly only seen by those with digital television. (The nadir was an item on the art of Leonardo, to accompany a segment about a garden 'inspired' by *The Da Vinci Code*.) The BBC should do half as much, twice as well; gush less and inform more. In short, follow the example of Chelsea exhibitors in the pursuit of excellence. The show deserves nothing less.

The Spectator
June 2007

In case you are wondering, after I mentioned the New Hall garden at the Chelsea Flower Show in last month's column, we did fine. It was enormous fun, we got a medal and plenty of publicity, and I will treasure the memory of distinguished Cambridge academics cheerfully handing out leaflets to visitors at a flower show. Chelsea show gardens are not always (and ours certainly was not) realistic models for people to copy in their own gardens; rather they have an underlying idea or theme capable of being realized in a horticultural setting.

I particularly enjoyed the way the visitors responded so enthusiastically to the idea behind ours – the link between the rare astronomical phenomenon of the transit of Venus and early botanical exploration – as well as the 'prismatic' or rainbow planting of perennials and bulbs, over which I had sweated blood.

Of the large show gardens, the one with the most interesting and well-realized theme was 'The Tribute to Linnaeus', designed by the Swedish garden designer Ulf Nordfjell and backed by the National Linnaeus Tercentenary Committee of Stockholm. Indeed, if it had not been for the tardy flowering of lilies and apple trees it must surely have won Best in Show. It was contemporary in feel, with a clean, uncluttered, linear layout, and the plants were mainly those natives which grew in Carl Linnaeus's garden at Hammarby in Sweden, such as silver birch, spruce, *Asarum europaeum*, *Fritillaria meleagris*, *Lilium martagon* var. *album* and *Linnaea borealis*.

The fact that the great man (born 23 May 1707) was a subject for a garden at Chelsea underlines his importance to gardeners, as well as botanists and natural scientists. His most lasting contribution was his adoption of the binomial (two names) system as a universal standard for designating plants and animals, which he set out in his *Species Plantarum* in 1753. (These names were Latin or Latinized; Latin was the educated man's *lingua franca* in the eighteenth century, and it has proved its usefulness for the modern global scientific community.) We take this consistent system of nomenclature entirely for granted, but we shouldn't forget that it cleared away longer and far more unwieldy descriptive names, called polynomials, which had been used by earlier naturalists to describe plants or animals. He personally named nearly six thousand plants. The simplicity and universal applicability of this system, coupled with Linnaeus's huge reputation, ensured that it was embraced internationally.

Linnaeus trained as a medical doctor, and was an intrepid and meticulous field botanist, discovering more than a hundred species in an epic journey to Lapland in 1732. He became Professor of Medicine and Botany in Uppsala in

1741, and died there in 1778. His urge to systematize the natural world put him in a long and distinguished line, which stretched back to Theophrastus in the fourth century BC. As well as adopting binomial nomenclature, he popularized a system of classifying plants by the sexual parts of their flowers, incidentally bringing condemnation down on his head from the Bishop of Carlisle for the 'gross prurience' of his mind. It was a leap forward, even if it did not survive very far into the nineteenth century.

Britons have a soft spot for Linnaeus, perhaps because his botanical, zoological and library collections were sold by his widow to an English naturalist, Sir James Edward Smith, who brought them to London. When Smith died, they were sold to the Linnean Society of London, of which he was a founder and the first President. This is the world's oldest biological society, dating from 1788, is housed in Burlington House, Piccadilly, and has 2,000 professional and amateur naturalist and scientist fellows. It was at the Linnean Society, on 1 July 1858, that Charles Darwin and Alfred Wallace first publicly expounded their theories on evolution.

Unlike many important innovators, Linnaeus was famous in his own day, and his spirit of enquiry, vision and energy remain an inspiration. These days, botanical taxonomists are strongly focused on the study of the DNA of plants, since this allows more accurate information on relatedness and evolution and, thereby, holds out vast possibilities for advancing medical and environmental research. These studies have been coordinated by the Angiosperm Phylogeny Group based at Kew Gardens, and led by Professor Mark Chase. To the layman, the relationships discovered by the close study of plant DNA seem sometimes most surprising. What gardener could have supposed that orchids and asparagus, or roses and nettles, were even distantly related? But, although systems of plant classification have changed over the centuries, binomial nomenclature survives – as the Costa Rican orchid *Masdevallia chasei*, named in honour of Mark Chase, bears witness. Linnaeus referred to his *Species*

Plantarum as 'the greatest achievement in the realm of science'. Overweening arrogance, or no more than the plain truth? You decide.

The Spectator
June 2003

'I don't mind admitting it, it was a rather clever wheeze. I managed to acquire a ticket for Press Day at Chelsea – the Monday, you know – by bringing up a plant for an award at the show. I asked my poor sister Pam to cut an armful of lilac from the Gatehouse Border, and I took it up with me in the train. (I left Pam at home, by the way, because the compost heaps needed turning urgently – I am not sure she would have enjoyed the trip, in any event, since the Underground gives her rampant clorstraphobia.) It is true, the judges wrote rather a terse comment on the card, saying that this plant first received the Award of Merit in 1911, but how was I to know that?

'Anyway, the important thing was that I was in on the Monday, able to move around as easily as can be, although the place was rather heaving with scruffy journalists such as that tiresome woman I told you about, Alison Buchanan her name is, who came to interview me once and was such a bore. Generally, though, I had a lovely day. First I had a word with the President, whom I bumped into (literally!!). He said not to worry; he was fine and it was surely his fault. He asked me if I were enjoying the show. Such lovely manners. But, there again, you know where you are with a baronet, as Arthur used to say, and he should have known! And, of course, if there is one thing better than a baronet, it is a baronet with a garden full of magnolias and camellias to die for. Unfortunately, he *is* rather tied up next spring, he tells me. So sad.

'After that, I dodged the showers and went to look at the show gardens. Goodness me, how extraordinary! One of them was apparently trying to depict a coral reef, using cabbages, primulas and proteas. Not sure it worked, although the wire octopus was rather jolly. The catalogue said: "The garden translates tropical subaquascape into terrestrial forms . . ." Well, who would have thought it?

'As for the garden designed by the little man who makes Hoovers somewhere in the Far East! You know the one I mean. He used to live near us, but has now bought an *enormous* house practically on the hard shoulder of the M4. For some reason, there was no green foliage in the garden at all, so it was all purple hedges and grey-blue cypresses, and as mournful as Arthur's funeral. It was called the Wrong Garden. Perhaps next year they will try to get it Right!!

'But I must say I was cheered by how well the gentry did this year. You can't keep 'em down, however much our so-called "government" tries: Xa Tollemache, Tom Stuart-Smith, Christopher Bradley-Hole . . . It was very cheering. I especially loved dear Tom's garden with that "flowery mead" of tellima and white honesty, *Iris sibirica* (such as we have here round the lake) and *Geranium* 'Johnson's Blue', although how he got his *Cornus kousa* to flower so early I will never know! It may look a bit grassy later in the year, I suppose, but at least he avoided putting dahlias next to apple trees in blossom as they did in the Sexuality Garden, or whatever it was called. I hope the Members keep their notebooks firmly in the pockets of their Pakkamacs tomorrow, because they are NOT going to learn very much from THAT one. By the way, Christopher told me that the glass cube pavilion in the Abu Dhabi Sheikh's garden was inspired by the structure of the salt molecule, and symbolizes desalination. Well, the things you see when you don't have a gun, as Nanny Rakehandle used to say!

'Quite a number of one's chums were there (goodness knows how!) and it was easy enough to avoid the so-called "celebrities" – Lionel Blair, Christopher Timothy, Jerry Hall, Ringo Starr and the like. They are not celebrities in my book, I can tell you, although I *was* pleased to nod to the Bishop of London. I am sorry I never glimpsed Michael (Hezza, of course!), who is usually there, he tells me. I wanted to tease him about the euro, about which he is always rather boot-faced, and ask him why there are no flowers in his garden!!

'Strangely, the sweetest people on Press Day were the garden photographers, I thought. Such poppets. I talked to dear Andrew Lawson, who was on the top of a stepladder snapping away. I am uncertain quite how he fell orf but he smiled very sweetly and said he always got muddy when he was photographing. He promised *faithfully* that he would come and snap the delphiniums when they are at their best in the Walled Garden . . . Between you and me, when he comes, I'm going to get him to take a picture of the two Westies in the wheelbarrow as well. Very naughty of me, I know, but wouldn't it be heavenly? . . .'

Guinevere, Lady Rakehandle, was on the telephone to a very old and dear friend, who sadly doesn't get out much any more.

8

FOREIGN PARTS

The Spectator
April 2004

When I was a child, I pestered my mother to take us to Longleat. In the end she agreed, pleased perhaps to think I was developing a precocious interest in Elizabethan architecture. In fact, I had longed – oh, easily for weeks – to see the newly installed lions in all their strange, foreign magnificence and, almost as much, to acquire a car sticker, bearing the legend 'We have seen the Lions of Longleat'. The sticker remained until the lion face faded, a frequent reminder of an extraordinary day.

This spring, something of that childish excitement returned to me. I have longed, not for weeks but for decades, to see the native flora of the western Cape in South Africa; ever since I was a student at Kew, in fact, when I caught a faint whiff of its glory, like the perfume of a woman who passes you in a shop doorway. In those Surrey glasshouses grew tender South African heaths and pelargoniums, and bulbs such as *Nerine sarniensis*, *Cyrtanthus elatus* (Scarborough lily), watsonias and moraeas. Outside, there were tubs of agapanthus, as well as amaryllis, tulbaghia and osteospermum in hot borders. These all spoke of landscapes vastly foreign but alluring. At the same period, the august Kirstenbosch Botanical Garden in Cape Town (set, most beautifully, in the shadow of Table Mountain) began to exhibit at the Chelsea Flower Show, stupefying the senses with exotic, colourful displays of proteas and restios. Finally, last month, thanks to the generosity of the National Botanical Institute, which runs the eight botanic gardens in South Africa, I got the chance to look at some of these plants in their native land.

It is a truism that the British Isles has the smallest and least spectacular, but best studied, flora in the world. We love it, but are conscious there are far greater riches elsewhere. Visiting the Cape underlines that strongly. The *fynbos* (pronounced 'faneboss') vegetation, which makes up four-fifths of what has been designated the Cape Floral Kingdom, and covers an area about the size of Portugal, hosts 8,600 plant species, 5,800 of which are endemic – that is, they grow naturally nowhere else in the world. The British Isles, on the other hand, which is three and a half times bigger, has 1,500 species (the same number as on Table Mountain alone), fewer than 20 of which are endemic, and about half of which are actually introductions. The numbers are hard to encompass, but they point to an astonishing biodiversity and, moreover, because of the high level of endemicity, a hugely threatened one.

The *fynbos* flora is so individual because of its geology. The soil is acid and desperately poor in nutrients. Very particular plants have evolved to survive the conditions: there are three main families – proteas, heaths (*Erica*) and Cape reeds (*Restio*) – together with geophytes, that is bulbs. The rain mainly comes in winter (June to August) and is heaviest in the west, and the *fynbos* is raked by fierce winds in summer. Plants have evolved to cope with periodic fires. Nothing in the landscape – unless encroached upon by alien species like wattles and pines – is taller than 6 feet / 1.75 metres. Even at the end of summer, when I was there, the colours, predominantly green and yellow, came from the evergreen shrubs; only on close inspection is it possible to discern the presence of flowering plants. Spring – September to December – is the most floriferous time in the *fynbos*, when everyone – not just botanists, ecologists and geeky gardeners like me – can revel in the rich variety in colour and form.

Perhaps surprisingly, I find I am pleased I cannot begin to grow most *fynbos* plants at home. Many simply won't thrive, even if you understand their requirements. Kew itself lost the trick of getting proteas to flower between 1826 and 1986. In British gardens, you will find that far more South African plants come from the temperate grassland 'veld' of the north and east. This is where crocosmias, most red-hot-pokers and schizostylis grow. But it was the very apartness of the *fynbos* flora which appealed to me so strongly. I could simply enjoy the sight of it, unfettered by that low-grade longing that gardeners feel at the sight of beautiful plants they do not grow. Envy was irrelevant, even bad taste.

The western Cape has long been popular with Britons as a winter sun destination. No doubt greater numbers will be lured this year by enthusiastic travel articles, written to coincide with the tenth anniversary of democracy, praising the wine, seafood, whales, birds and spectacular landscapes. I hope those who come will drive out from Cape Town to the Cape of Good Hope Nature Reserve, not just to see the baboons, the cliffs and the South Atlantic Ocean, but to travel through a landscape of such variety and splendour that it must live long in the memory. No need for any 'We have seen the Cape Floral Kingdom' sticker, believe me.

Daily Telegraph
4 November 2006

If we British gardeners have a fault, it is a too-ready assumption that we have the best climate for gardening, the best gardeners and the best gardens in the world. Smug, or what? But, half a world away, in the southern hemisphere, is a botanical garden that ranks amongst the very best on earth. For my money, it is quite unsurpassed in the quality and magnificence of its setting, its plants and the experience a day spent there affords the visitor.

For some bizarre reason, Kirstenbosch Botanical Garden is only the second-most visited tourist attraction in Cape Town, beaten by the thoroughly overrated Waterfront; nevertheless, few Britons pass through the Western Cape without a trip into the suburb of Newlands to see it. At Kirstenbosch,

Table Mountain – that great ancient outcrop of sandstone, which so dominates the skyline of Cape Town – seems so close you can touch it. In fact, you can, since the garden extends into the eastern slopes of the mountain, and there are very popular walks to the summit.

This area of the Cape was colonized early: Stone Age remains have been found in the garden, while the pastoralist Khoi Khoi people lived here for at least two thousand years. In 1660, Jan van Riebeeck, the first Dutch Governor of the Cape, caused a hedge of wild almond to be planted to mark the boundary of the Dutch settlement, and protect the cattle belonging to the settlers from the Khoi Khoi. Amazingly, part of his hedge survives in the garden today and is preserved as a national monument. In the late nineteenth century, Cecil Rhodes bought the land, and bequeathed it on his death to the people of South Africa. But it was not until 1913 that the botanical garden was established.

The estate runs to 1,305 acres/528 hectares and includes evergreen Afromontane forest on the slopes of Table Mountain, but the cultivated garden is a more manageable 100 acres/40 hectares. All the plants grown are native to South Africa and most are of the extraordinary, wonderful, endemic (geographically specific) and threatened *fynbos* flora from the Cape. This is a winter rainfall area, but the very warmest and driest north-facing slope in the garden is home to plants, many of them succulent, which arise from the summer rainfall areas of southern Africa, such as the Drakensberg Mountains in KwaZulu-Natal.

A real highlight for me is the Protea Garden (the king protea is the symbol of South Africa). Proteas and the related leucadendrons are at their best in winter and spring, and are followed by summer-flowering pincushions (*Leucospermum*). To see the Cape sugarbirds dipping their curved beaks into the flowers is an unforgettable treat. Kirstenbosch is also home to the guinea-fowl-like Cape francolin, the glorious iridescent-plumaged lesser double-collared sunbird and the spotted eagle owl. If you are lucky, you may also catch sight of a mongoose.

As remarkable as the protea family, perhaps, are the cycads, 'living fossil' survivors of an ancient group of gymnosperms, planted here nearly a hundred years ago, in the Cycad Amphitheatre. These huge plants, with their palm-like fronds and female cones like great fat sponge fingers, are an impressive sight, doubly precious since they are now so rare in the wild.

For those of us not brought up with South African plants, as fascinating as anything are the educational gardens, such as the Useful Plants Garden, where so many medicinal plants still used in southern Africa are grown, together with the Water-Wise Garden (lack of water is an enduring, pressing preoccupation for South Africans). There are gardens which show indigenous plants that have become a nuisance when exported, as well as aliens that are a problem in South Africa.

Should it rain, there is the Botanical Society Conservatory, where plants which cannot be grown outside in the Cape are planted, especially those glorious ones from the desert, high mountain peaks and shady forests. The centrepiece is a baobab tree, a plant imbued with so many magical powers in Africa.

Kirstenbosch is held in great affection by Capetonians, as for almost a century it has been a backdrop to their lives. Through good times and bad, people have played, flirted and strolled along its shady paths or lain in the sun on the Main Lawn, where popular concerts are held on summer evenings (December to March). It is a safe and quiet haven from the busy, sometimes alarming, city close by.

It should not be forgotten, however, that it is also a scientific institution with an international reputation. At the Research Centre at Kirstenbosch, scientists study taxonomy, ecology, conservation, conservation farming, global change, desertification and horticulture. There is a DNA bank and a seed bank. In short, Kirstenbosch is South Africa's Kew. Yet, so diverse is the flora of this country, that there are no fewer than eight botanical gardens in South Africa, under the banner of the South African National Biodiversity Institute: three in the Cape, two in Gauteng and one in KwaZulu-Natal, Mpumalanga and Free

State. Any British gardener interested in growing South African plants can do much worse than make a leisurely tour of these gardens. Or they can just enjoy them for what they are, rich repositories of the natural world.

The Spectator
April 2006

British gardeners are often accused of being parochial, and we rarely make much attempt to defend ourselves against the charge. We think it is probably true but wonder what anyone expects, considering the advantages of climate, soil and geography we enjoy and how beautiful our gardens can be as a result. It is scarcely surprising if we rarely see much reason to raise our eyes above, and beyond, the horizon. We can rely on nearly five thousand gardens opening their gates to us, for charity or profit, at least once a year, not to mention our own gardens to enjoy each day. Who can blame us, we say, if we lack a proper appreciation of what is going on elsewhere?

It is slightly shaming to say it, but only when I am abroad does this forcibly strike me. I have just come back from a short visit to California, which has an awesomely rich native flora as well as a substantial number of fascinating and beautiful gardens, the older ones influenced by European ideas and using European plants, while the modern ones are more likely to contain indigenous ones. There are 6,000 species of native Californian plants, many of them endemic, occurring in a great number of ecological niches, under the general headings of woodland, coastal, wetland, mountain and desert. (Of course, the vegetation types are far, far more complex and interesting than that short list implies.) The range of topography in the state is so great that it influences the flora more even than the latitude. Part of California, especially near the coast, has a 'Mediterranean' climate, with warm, relatively wet winters and long, dry, hot summers, while inland it is continental, with a much greater difference between winter and summer temperatures.

California has fostered dozens of garden designers of real note, including the hugely admired Thomas Church, working after the Second World War, while currently there are a number, in particular Nancy Goslee Power, Ron Lutsko and Bernard Trainor. They are rather more interested in ecological planting than Church was. Their ideas, especially on how to use wildflowers, have had some influence on British garden designers but, until recently, rather less on the average British gardener. We seem to need to see foreign ideas filtered through the consciousness of prominent British gardeners, before we get the hang of the plot.

However, that *has* been happening of late. A number of British contemporary designers, influenced by the New Naturalism movement, are using plants to create something resembling 'natural' plant communities. Moreover, influential garden owners are experimenting with the use of foreign vegetation types, particularly those of the Californian coastal strip and the Chaparral, as well as the Mid-West American prairie, the Mediterranean maquis and garrigue, South African winter rainfall areas, even arid areas and desert. Parts of gardens, planted to resemble these habitats, can be seen in a number of gardens presently open to the public.

There is both a Cretan garden and an African one at the Garden House, Buckland Monachorum, in Devon, developed by Keith Wiley before he left to run his Wildside Plants nursery in 2003. The late Christopher Lloyd, influenced by the experimental work on prairie plantings done by Dr James Hitchmough of Sheffield University, brought back seed from Minnesota for his last garden project, an American-style prairie at Great Dixter in East Sussex. At the Old Vicarage, East Ruston, quite close to the sea in Norfolk, Alan Gray and Graham Robeson have made not only a Mediterranean garden and a South African one but also, fascinatingly, a 'desert wash', designed to mimic the Arizonan desert after twice-yearly heavy rainfall, using some of the plants which can survive in that harsh environment. And at Elmstead Market, in Essex, Beth Chatto has made a highly successful, Mediterranean gravel garden out of the erstwhile nursery car park.

Some may argue that these are classy pastiches, and that these gardeners might have been better employed perfecting 'the English garden look', since it is suited to our climate, and usually successful. To do so, however, is to ignore the fact that this climate is changing, and summer drought in the south and east of England is now the spectre at the feast. Much of this experimentation with foreign plant communities is simply a considered, informed response to that. If it is possible, as Beth Chatto has shown us that it is, to grow a mixture of southern European, Californian and South African plants, in a self-sustaining, self-perpetuating community, with no watering after the plants have become established, why, gardeners in the south-east would be bonkers not even to consider following suit.

Moreover, these attempts at developing plant communities, as they might be seen in landscapes abroad, seem to me a homage paid by British gardeners to the variety and quality of other countries' native flora. Indeed, you might say that British gardens have always paid that homage. Once it was the Middle East, the Himalayas and China, now it is California, the Mid-West and Australia. Perhaps we are not so parochial after all?

The Spectator
May 2004

British gardens look the way they do for a number of impressively diverse reasons: politics, fashion, culture, society, creative energy, geology and climate. These imperatives, when connected, have produced one of the great glories of our civilization. There is one more aspect, however, which is the work of only a small number of individuals. That aspect is plant exploration abroad.

Our gardens are not little parcels of native landscape, for the simple reason that they are full of exotic plants plucked from foreign habitats and persuaded to thrive in our climate. These exotics have mainly been introduced by plant hunters. Whole families of gardenworthy plants have arrived here by those means. Without plant exploration, we would have no rhododendrons, gentians, magnolias, meconopsis, daphnes or Douglas firs. Our primulas would be restricted to the cowslip and primrose, our irises consist of the gladdon and the yellow water flag and our conifers be limited to the Scots pine and yew.

Plant hunters risked (and still do risk, since plant hunting has far from died out, even if it has partly changed in character) their health, wealth and lives to collect plants in other countries, often in very difficult circumstances. Gardeners are, not surprisingly, fascinated by these people, which is why the centenary of George Forrest's first plant-hunting expedition in 1904 is being celebrated by the publication of a book, a lecture day in April and a number of commemorative events in those large gardens which have benefited particularly from Forrest introductions, such as the Royal Botanic Garden, Edinburgh, Exbury and Caerhays.

Plant hunting has always been so difficult, if rewarding, and required such strength of character and determination, because our gardens require plants hardy against frost yet able to withstand wind and wet. In other countries, that often means they have to come from mountainous regions above 4,900 feet/1,500 metres. George Forrest's seven expeditions between 1904 and 1932 (when he died of a heart attack whilst shooting game) were conducted in north-west Yunnan, close to the borders with Burma and Tibet, in that vertiginously mountainous area bisected longitudinally by the Rivers Salween, Mekong and Yangtze, and at altitudes ranging from 3,280 to 16,400 feet/1,000 to 5,000 metres. Western China is one of the most floristically rich temperate regions in the world, and is still the stamping ground for adventurous British plant hunters, such as Peter Cox, Roy Lancaster and Chris Grey-Wilson.

The son of a Scottish draper, Forrest had been, amongst other things, a gold prospector in Australia before he settled to work in the Herbarium at the Royal Botanic Garden at Edinburgh. When he was thirty-one, the Regius Keeper, Sir Isaac Bayley Balfour, was approached by Arthur Bulley, a Liverpool cotton broker who had established a nursery at his garden at Ness (now the Ness Botanic Gardens). He wanted a plant hunter to look for gardenworthy plants in areas of China not yet even surveyed. Bayley Balfour suggested Forrest: 'He is a strongly built fellow and seems to me of the right grit for a collector.'

On his first expedition, which lasted three years, Forrest found the autumn gentian, *Gentiana sino-ornata*, but nearly lost his life when he and some French missionaries, with whom he had been staying, were forced to flee by warlike Tibetan lamas. The French were murdered and their hearts torn out and he was hunted mercilessly for nine days. He eventually escaped, thanks to his fitness and resourcefulness, including taking his boots off so that he could not be tracked.

Bulley paid for the first two expeditions, but the third was financed by J.C. Williams of Caerhays Castle in Cornwall. Then it was the turn of the Royal Horticultural Society and a 'Syndicate of Gentlemen', which included Williams and Reginald Cory of Dyffryn. Forty-six well-heeled garden owners sponsored his last expedition in 1930. These were large and well-organized ventures, using native helpers to collect plants or seed. On Forrest's last expedition, 300 pounds/135 kilograms of seed was sent home.

In all, he collected 31,000 'immaculately annotated' dried specimens, of which more than 5,000 were rhododendrons. He introduced to cultivation some of our very finest woodland garden shrubs: *Rhododendron sino-grande*; *R. griersonianum* (the parent of many important hybrids such as 'Elizabeth'); the ground-hugging *R. forrestii*; *Camellia saluenensis*, which Williams crossed with

C. japonica to produce the famous *C.* × *williamsii* hybrids; and *Pieris formosa* var. *forrestii*. Amongst perennials, as well as the wonderful (and easy) blue *Gentiana sino-ornata*, there was *Primula bulleyana*, *P. malacoides* and *P. forrestii*. It is no exaggeration to say that the twentieth-century 'woodland garden' developed as a result of Forrest's introductions. His success was reinforced by the plant introductions of Reginald Farrer, Frank Ludlow, George Sheriff and Frank Kingdon Ward.

A bald list of plants gives no hint of the fascination of plant hunting: the romance, the fear, the fatigue, the discomfort, the loneliness, the disappointments and the excitement of finding something previously unknown and beautiful. Unlike Kingdon Ward, Forrest wrote no books, only articles in gardening periodicals. But the plants growing in gardens are memorial enough.

The Spectator
November 2005

The natural curiosity of gardeners means that we want always to know something of where our garden plants came from, and how we came by them. We are endlessly fascinated by the lives and exploits of plant hunters. It was ever thus. For a couple of centuries there has been a literary sub-genre devoted to the subject: books written by plant explorers – I am thinking of Reginald Farrer and Frank Kingdon Ward, in particular – who wrote well enough to enthral and excite an audience stuck at home. Plant hunters acquired a reputation for being eccentric, independent-minded, sometimes self-indulgent, but always interesting, audacious and driven.

These days, books about plant hunters are generally either historical in emphasis, such as Dr Toby Musgrave's *The Plant Hunters*, or part personal, part historical, such as Christian Lamb's *From the Ends of the Earth*, with few plant hunters writing of their experiences for the general reader, an exception being Roy Lancaster (*A Plantsman in Nepal*). This emphasis on the historical means that it is easy to gain the impression that the days of richly productive plant collecting in remote and rugged places are now gone.

In fact that is not so. There is plenty of plant hunting still going on; it is just rather more controlled and focused, and much less often freelance or self-indulgent. The emphasis is on contributions to science and to horticulture; self-aggrandisement is frowned upon. You have to delve a bit to discover who these modern British collectors are, since they are usually rather self-effacing, but they are scarcely less intrepid or skilled than their forebears, nevertheless: Roy Lancaster, Christopher Grey-Wilson, Christopher Brickell, Peter and Kenneth Cox, Martyn Rix, James Compton, John d'Arcy, Bleddyn and Sue Wynn-Jones, Ronald McBeath, Phillip Cribb, to mention just some of them.

In earlier times, plant hunters were either employed by botanic gardens or nurseries, such as Veitch's of Exeter, or they were free spirits, like Reginald Farrer, who collected principally for themselves, with perhaps some financial help from friends who took seeds in return. Permission was not always sought from the country where the collecting was to be done, for official institutions did not sometimes exist. Plant hunters were often exposed to danger from hostile native people (in the case of Farrer usually warlike Tibetan monks), as well as wild animals and natural catastrophes. Most plant exploration, these days, is done under the auspices of botanical establishments or plant societies. Nurseries no longer send paid plant hunters abroad, although the Wynn-Joneses, owners of Crûg Farm Nursery in north Wales, are famous travellers, having collected everywhere from Guatemala to South Korea.

For the last twenty-five years at least, no *bona fide* collector has dreamt of collecting without the permission of the authorities in the country to be explored or without CITES clearance, and usually works with the active cooperation of the local botanical institution as well. Indeed, the international cooperation between scientific establishments tends to be close, thanks as much as anything to the universal camaraderie engendered by the Internet.

Trips these days rarely last more than a few weeks, as a result of swift international flights, long-wheel-based Land Rovers and the cost-consciousness of scientific institutions. The modern plant hunter has benefits denied his predecessors (Gore-tex, digital cameras and satellite navigation) but the nitty-gritty of plant hunting and collection – pressing specimens, changing the drying paper of plants already pressed, writing notes and diaries, cleaning and labelling seed – at the end of each hard day is the same as ever. Carelessness about discomfort, meticulous attention to detail, inexhaustible optimism, patience and sound botanical knowledge: these are the marks of a good plant hunter, of whatever era. Protecting health in unpromising regions and dreadful weather remains the same – keeping your feet dry as well as your mind clear when crossing gorges on a high rope bridge, dodging rock falls and avoiding road accidents, bandits and wild animals.

Back home, the field notes must be printed, herbarium specimens sent to botanical gardens, seed cleaned and live plants, if any, distributed. Those of possible gardenworthiness have to be sent to nurseries for evaluation, naming, bulking up and eventual sale. Contemporary plant collectors are responsible for introducing such beautiful garden plants as *Corydalis flexuosa* 'China Blue', *Daphne bholua* 'Gurkha', *Veronica peduncularis* 'Georgia Blue', *Actaea taiwanensis* and *Salvia patens* 'Guanajuato'.

In one very important particular, however, contemporary plant hunting differs from that which went on before the last world war. The accelerating destruction of habitats, and the pressing need to conserve rare and endangered species, have given this task a new urgency. You may not hear a great deal about modern plant hunters but, by golly, we need them.

The Spectator
March 2008

If you are an assiduous buyer of plants, you will know that there are a quite a number of foreign-bred plants for sale in our nurseries. This has become more obvious in recent years, since the nomenclature rules have changed. These days, a plant should be sold under its original name – if it is in a language using Roman script, at least. *Penstemon* 'Garnet', for example, should now be labelled *Penstemon* 'Andenken an Friedrich Hahn'. It may not be as snappy, but it is right and proper, since this penstemon was bred in Germany.

If you are a keen grower of clematis, you will certainly know that there are a number of excellent garden varieties with Polish names: 'Błekitny Anioł', 'Kardynał Wyszyński', 'Generał Sikorski', 'Warszawska Nike', 'Emilia Plater' 'Jan Paweł II', and 'Matka Siedliska', for example. (They will probably be misspelled, since nursery labelling machines don't do diacritic marks, but they are still obviously Polish.) However, you may not know that all these clematis – whose names often celebrate great patriotic luminaries of the Polish church, such as Pope John Paul II and Cardinal Wyszyński, or famous military events in Poland's history, like Monte Cassino and Westerplatte – have all been bred by a Jesuit priest, Brother Stefan Franczak, living quietly in a monastery in a Warsaw suburb.

In his youth, Brother Stefan studied animal breeding at university, but joined the Society of Jesus in 1948, aged thirty-one. In 1950, his superiors put him in charge of the 3.5-acre/1.5-hectare kitchen garden next to the monastery. When it looked as if the Communist authorities might annexe the garden for public building, the Jesuits decided to make it into an ornamental garden, open to the public. In time, this garden became known throughout Poland.

Brother Stefan began actively to breed clematis in the 1960s, after he had found some self-sown seedlings in the garden. Amateur plant breeders are often exceptional people, with energy, patience and acute observational powers but Brother Stefan stands out, even in such company. His clematis are remarkable for their bright colours, good form and profuse, extended flowering, as well as disease resistance and hardiness. He would observe seedlings for up to twelve years before being satisfied enough to register them officially; to date, there are more than sixty registered.

In 1996, the garden was reduced to 1.25 acres/0.5 hectares, after a church was built on part of it. Nevertheless, when I visited it five years ago, it still felt substantial, and I was struck by its distinct and restful charm. Clematis were everywhere, mainly trained up vertical metal reinforcing rods, and there were large beds of irises and hemerocallis (day lilies), the other two genera on which he worked. Brother Stefan was ill in a nursing home at the time, but I met his assistant, who showed me his 'stud books'. It is impossible not to make a mental connection here with the Augustinian monk Brother Gregor Mendel, who published his historic work on genetics in Brno, Czechoslovakia, only ten years before Brother Stefan was born in Jeziorna, Poland. And it is touching to think of him working away in obscurity in the grim Communist days, producing beautiful plants with openly subversive names, for the glory of his God and his country.

He became known in Britain, after Jim Fisk, a clematis nurseryman, introduced his 'Jan Paweł II' ('John Paul II'), at the Chelsea Flower Show in 1982. Since then, most of his selections have arrived here thanks to his friend Szczepan Marczyński, who was the man who showed me round the monastery garden. Szczepan is another impressive Pole, who was once an important Solidarnosc activist, and is also a breeder of fine clematis, including 'Barbara', 'Jerzy Popiełuszko', 'Lech Wałęsa' and 'Solidarność'. He has a progressively run nursery at Pruszków, outside Warsaw, where he grows more than a hundred different types of climber (which can be viewed at his exemplary website, www.clematis.com.pl). The latest Brother Stefan clematis to be introduced is

'Slowianka', and Szczepan says that there are likely to be more in the future. The monk also registered more than a hundred varieties of hemerocallis, most of them growing at Wojsawice, a branch of the Wrocław Botanical Garden.

Five years ago, the monastery garden was nearly lost altogether, when Brother Stefan's superiors wanted to make it into a plain park. Then sixty representations by clematis enthusiasts from across the world helped persuade the Rector (who cannot have known what hit him) not to do something so drastic, and Brother Stefan was allowed to keep a small garden for as long as he could manage it. Recently, however, he has become very frail, and is in a Jesuit retirement home.* The monastery garden may now be almost all grassed over, but the fruits of this good man's labours are to be seen every season all over the temperate world.

* *In March 2009, Brother Stefan was awarded the Commander's Cross of the Order of Polonia Restituta for his outstanding work, by the President of Poland.*

9

NATURAL AND UNNATURAL ILLS

'Borderlines', *Daily Telegraph*
1 September 2007

In the late 1970s, when I was training to be a gardener, entomology and plant pathology featured prominently as subjects in the curriculum, even meriting separate exams. This was hardly surprising, since an understanding of pests and diseases, and how to prevent or mitigate their worst effects, was and is vital for a gardener, professional or amateur. There was, I recall, a great deal of emphasis on what pesticides could be employed to combat which pests and diseases and I diligently learned their unmemorable names by rote.

How times have changed! Most of those chemicals are not now available to professional gardeners, let alone amateurs, any more. This has usually been because the research needed to provide data to comply with the Plant Protection Products Regulations was too costly to bother with, rather than because they were deleterious to health. However, even if they were still around, I doubt whether they would be used that much. Most gardeners I know, especially younger ones, react to any suggestion that they might use a spray, as if one had used a very rude word in public. The majority of gardeners, whether they call themselves 'organic' or not, never now use pesticides on vegetables and fruit at all, and rarely, if at all, on anything in the flower borders either. The hardest habit to kick, especially if you have a large garden, is giving up weedkillers, to clean paths and battle with promiscuous, overbearing perennial weeds like dock, hogweed and couch grass.

If gardening is not to be too hard a physical slog, 'organic' gardeners need to become at least reasonably proficient botanists, plant physiologists, pathologists and entomologists. Botany helps you with the life cycles of weeds, plant physiology promotes an understanding of how to nourish plants, without using artificial fertilizers, plant pathology gives an insight into providing conditions where diseases can't thrive, while zoology promotes an understanding of pests, and the beneficial creatures which predate them.

Here are just a few examples to show what I mean. In order to thwart the codling moth, I put up traps in the apple trees in May, which lure males to a sticky end with the use of a synthetic pheromone (sexual attractant). In early winter, I wind sticky grease bands round the trunks of fruit trees, because female winter moths, which are wingless, climb up trees to lay their eggs in crevices. Laying horticultural fleece over carrot seedlings prevents the egress of carrot fly, which find the carrots by the scent of the leaves.

The problem with all this virtuous, thoughtful and informed activity is that you can undermine the look of the garden, sometimes quite seriously. I am not wild about the CDs hanging from string in the vegetable garden to scare off the pigeons, but even worse is the plastic-sheeted wooden frame which, each year between November and May, covers a fan-trained peach tree, growing against a wall on one side of the flower garden. This keeps the tree dry and so prevents the germination of the spores of peach leaf curl, a fungal disease which seriously weakens the tree and its fruit-bearing capacity. It works an absolute treat, and we enjoy tremendous crops of peaches each year, but not even I would say it looked attractive. Hmmph.

'Borderlines', *Daily Telegraph*
6 November 2004

I was staring out of the kitchen window in a more than usually vacant way the other day, when my attention was caught by the movement of a grey squirrel under the table on the terrace. It had a large walnut sticking out of its mouth. It looked left, then right, then left again, for all the world as if it were a grey version of Mr Tufty demonstrating the kerb drill. It then tippy-toed, in that cagey way squirrels have, to one of the terracotta pots near the French windows, and leapt on to it, amongst the winter pansies. It then buried the walnut for the winter in the special peat-free, sustainable, save-the-planet compost into which the pansies, and a great many bulbs in several layers, had recently been planted. Considering how full the pot was of tulip, narcissus and crocus, it made a fine job of finding space for the walnut. When it had finished, it carefully patted the pansy heads back into place again. (I am sure I did not dream that.)

We only see a squirrel in the garden in the autumn, when it is lured by the scent of the cultivated hazels in the nuttery, and the walnuts in our neighbour's paddock. This is the same squirrel, I would bet, which a month ago, and much to my fury, ran along the fence rail at one side of the paddock, with one of my treasured filberts in its insolent mouth. Since netting the shrubs is an impossible task (and, anyway, who ever said a squirrel couldn't bite through netting?), we have had to harvest as many cobs and filberts as possible just before the squirrel gets to them, and certainly before they are properly ripe. Left in a bowl for a couple of weeks, however, they have ripened and sweetened well enough to please us. We have no choice, in any event.

Squirrels are a menace to gardeners: there is no doubt about it. They don't just go for nuts, but they eat top and soft fruit as well, and also flower buds and shoots. They are supposed, although I have never seen it, to remove plant labels to sharpen their teeth, which does show a certain sophistication. The squirrel has left the fruit cage alone so far, and wasps are definitely more of a problem amongst the fruit trees in the orchard, but the nuttery is very fair game to *Sciurus carolinensis*. When my own walnut trees are large enough to bear fruit, I suppose I shall have to put up metal baffles round the trunks, as squirrel bafflers.

Every autumn, at this time, my husband threatens to buy an air gun to despatch the squirrel. But, somehow, it never quite happens. The reason has nothing to do with soft heartedness, since neither of us is under the illusion that animals are really humans in furry disguise and the grey squirrel is an alien and invasive species, as bad in its way as Japanese knotweed. However, we are well aware that squirrels are territorial and, if we lose this one, we will probably just acquire another. And, although the grey squirrel is an infuriating creature and can be a nest raider, it is hard to dislike it as much as, say, a magpie or a crow, somehow. As for its habit of burying nuts for another day, I shall be almost grateful to it, if a walnut seedling appears with the tulips next May.

The Spectator
5 April 2008

In the last few months, I have idly watched the slow spread of a green moss in a very shady place on the north side of our house and, then, the seeding into the moss of small native plants, in particular hairy bitter cress. Usually, I am ruthless in removing this cress when I find it in the borders, because it is such a profligate seeder, but I let it stay, fascinated by its capacity to colonize what was rather a hostile environment. It intrigues me what chooses to seed itself where, plants often contradicting my own pre-conceived ideas as to what is possible.

Then, one day, I had had enough, and deliberately destroyed this embryo eco-system. It was no big deal, of course, for we gardeners do it all the time: it's called weeding. The only difference was that this moss and hairy bitter cress had been growing on the back windowsill of my navy-blue, L reg., 1.8 litre Volvo 440 Li; if I was going to have any chance at all of selling the old car, I had to give it a good clean and wash. But I felt a pang, nevertheless.

The Spectator
August 2004

The daily walk I take in the countryside loses something of its pleasure in June and July. The sight of numerous small trees in the roadside hedgerows, with their branches rigid and leafless or with sick, yellow foliage, causes me a sharp stab of regret. These young trees are suckers from the roots of dead English elms (*Ulmus procera*), and the closely related, smooth-leaved elm (*U. minor*), which survive only until they are mature enough to grow bark, which they do after about ten years. Under the bark bores the elm bark beetle, infecting the tree with the fatal fungus, Dutch elm disease, as it goes.

I am old enough to remember the worst ever outbreak of Dutch elm disease in this country, in the early 1970s, of which these hedgerow suckers are some of the poor survivors. In the paddock next to our garden in Oxfordshire, there were six fine trees and, as a child, I would lie in bed on summer mornings, listening to the rooks cawing raggedly in their tops. One day, a tree surgeon arrived to inject the trees with a fungicide, fruitlessly as it turned out, so he returned to cut them all down. In all, at least 20 million trees died across the country: English and smooth-leaved elms in a swathe from Plymouth through the Midlands to East Anglia (including those that Constable had painted in Dedham Vale) and wych elms (*Ulmus glabra*), which rarely sucker, further north. The landscape changed. The nation mourned. Only in the north of Scotland, thanks to the beetle's dislike of Scotch mist, did mature wych elms survive in any numbers.

Since the 1920s, when there was a lesser outbreak of DED, continuous efforts have been made to find genetically resistant or immune clones, or to breed resistant hybrids, using not only European but Asian and American elm species as well. The Dutch and the Americans have been especially assiduous, the former perhaps stung by being blamed, wrongly, for the spread of the disease.

There have been several false dawns, with introductions such as 'Dodoens' turning out to be less than satisfactory in the end.

Recently, however, there have been promising developments. At the Chelsea Flower Show this year, two resistant elms were on offer: a clone of the American elm (*Ulmus americana*), named 'The Princeton Elm', propagated from trees which have survived in the town of Princeton. This is now available from Knoll Gardens. And there was 'New Horizon', a small, compact tree from Hillier Nurseries, which is a cross made in the United States between the Japanese and Siberian elms.

These are desirable trees for botanic gardens, public parks, streets and large private gardens. However, they are not native elms, or even crosses between native elms, and I, for one, would feel queasy about planting any of them in the countryside.

But there may be good news on that score, too. The Hampshire branch of Butterfly Conservation has been running a number of trials in its three reserves, to try to establish what elms are suitable for countryside planting and sufficiently resistant to DED to act as a long-term food source for the extremely picky white-letter hairstreak butterfly, whose decline has been dramatic since the loss of the elms. Its recent report praises the impossibly named *Ulmus* × *Lutece R. Nanguen*. This is a hybrid, derived from the three European species, which in form and leaf looks similar to the English elm. It appears to be fast growing, except on heavy wet soils, and is very hardy. So far it has proved itself 'immune' to DED, although only more time will tell that for certain.

More exciting, because on a much greater scale, is the research work being done by a coalition of conservation bodies, including the Natural History Museum. This grouping has established an Elm Map initiative, to pinpoint the position of mature elms all over the country, by recruiting walkers to identify them. Last year, Elm Walks during the Ramblers' 'Welcome to Walking Week' in September brought 441 sightings. Not only are mature trees important hosts for rare butterflies, lichens, mosses and fungi, but they are likely to be resistant or even possibly immune to DED. The Conservation Foundation has already taken cuttings from some of these trees, and given them to a nursery to propagate and build up stocks. So it is just possible that, one day, my summer walks will once more be free from care and regret.

The Spectator
January 2004

SOD it, SOD it, SOD IT. How many garden owners of unimpeachable respectability must have allowed themselves the relief of an expletive or three as they read the news headlines last month about Sudden Oak Death or *Phytophthora ramorum*? No doubt, like me, they have been trying since March 2002, when the news first broke that it had arrived in this country, to pretend that life could go on as normal; that a disease which might be devastating tanoak forests in California and Oregon had so far only touched a few rhododendrons and viburnums in nurseries and large 'heritage' gardens here. But it was the announcement that SOD had infected a holm oak, a beech and a southern red oak – and so might just turn out to be as devastating to the look of the landscape as the outbreak of Dutch Elm Disease in the early 1970s – which really put the wind up us all.

If you are not interested in plant pathology, or could not be persuaded to be, I suggest you turn the page now. For everyone else, *Phytophthora ramorum* is a fungal pathogen, which causes three diseases – Sudden Oak Death, Ramorum Dieback and Ramorum Leaf Blight. It was first identified in California and northern Europe ten years ago and, since it appeared in Britain in 2002, has been found in nurseries all over the country, having been imported from the Continent. It is spread in rain splash, in contaminated soil or by human or animal agency. It affects rhododendron and viburnum principally, but also a number of ericaceous shrubs like kalmia, camellia and vaccinium, as well as lilac and yew. On rhododendron, it causes twig and leaf browning and dieback, while viburnums are struck on the stem just above soil level and sometimes die. Trees develop cankers and ooze red or black sap from the bark. It has a number of spore types, both asexual and sexual; the two mating types are A1 (seen in Europe) and A2 (the US).

Gardens where an infected plant has been found so far (Heligan, Wisley and Lanhydrock, for example) have all been 'woodland' gardens on acid soil. The National Trust and other large garden owners are understandably very twitchy: important and venerable individual plants are at risk, much needed garden visitors may inadvertently spread the disease and these gardens often adjoin natural woodland.

Preliminary research suggests that the native wych elm is also susceptible to this pathogen. More worryingly, so are beech and the chestnuts, as well as Lawson cypress, although that thug Leyland cypress unfortunately is not. Douglas fir and Sitka spruce, both important commercial timber trees, are at risk. *Rhododendron ponticum*, a weed if ever there was one, is highly susceptible but that is less than no consolation, since it provides the shrubby understorey in many woods on acid soils, and can provide what the scientists call inoculum to infect native tree and shrub species.

The Plant Health Division of Defra, as well as Forest Research (part of the Forestry Commission) have projects under way, to study the action and spread of the disease, as well as assess the risks to nurseries, gardens and the wider landscape. Surveys of outbreak sites and large gardens are being carried out. Checks at ports have been stepped up. The problem is that this disease is impossible to pick out in small plants on nurseries and can also be masked temporarily by fungicides; only laboratory tests are conclusive. If you are worried that you might buy an infected rhododendron which won't show symptoms until it is nicely ensconced in your garden amongst all your other rhododendrons, all I can say is that nurseries are being inspected twice as often as usual, and infected plants destroyed.

There are a number of – as yet unresolved – fears clutching us by the throat. In particular, are the spores carried on the air, as well as in water and on boots, and will the A2 mating type appear in Europe and reproduce sexually with the A1 strain? If that happened, the progeny might be better adapted to the conditions or more aggressive, which is partly why there are EC-wide emergency measures now in force, preventing plant and timber imports from affected areas of the United States. So far, A1 has been found in only one site in Europe. Unfortunately, the authorities have legitimate worries about illicit imports of plants without 'passports' from some European countries.

With the current state of knowledge, the Royal Horticultural Society is not recommending that we gardeners modify our behaviour, except to urge us to buy from reputable sources, and check already planted shrubs for signs of disease, comparing them to the photographs on Defra's website. If *Phytopthora ramorum* is suspected, we must get in touch with the local office of the Plant Health and Seeds Inspectorate, since this is a notifiable disease.

It is a pious hope to think that keen eyes, swift analysis and strict phytosanitary procedures will stop the disease spreading, but it is possible that *Phytophthora ramorum* will in the end be confined to localized outbreaks. Rhododendrons can regrow and preliminary research shows our native oaks to be less susceptible than American species. They are also more genetically heterogeneous than elms, because the latter naturally spread by suckering. Certainly, the long-established and well-known *Phytophthora* root rots, which can weaken or kill a wide variety of species, are a nuisance rather than devastating to gardeners and foresters, and are controlled in nurseries. It is 150 years since *Phytophthora infestans*, potato blight, fundamentally changed the history of these islands and that of the United States. Surely, we have learned a few lessons since then?

The Spectator
15 March 2008

The story of old Mrs Foster, who lived in the village where I was brought up, and who contracted lockjaw whilst cutting her raspberry canes, has remained with me since childhood. This event acquired almost mythic status in my mind, since no one saw fit to enlighten me further. Why would she want to cut her raspberry canes, anyway and, even if she did, why would that give her this unexplained affliction? Was she a gossip, and therefore could this be seen as an improvement? Most importantly, what happened to her? No one ever said.

You would have thought, after this cautionary experience, that I would have had a healthy respect for tetanus and its mysterious, but obviously baleful, effects. Yet, when I airily enquired of the GP surgery nurse how long it was since I had been given an anti-tetanus injection, she rather less airily replied: 'Seventeen years. And' – there was no denying the accusatory tone in her voice – 'you a gardener, too.' I went home with a sore arm and a chastened spirit, determined that I should never again take the risk of suffering old Mrs Foster's fate – whatever that had been.

'Borderlines', *Daily Telegraph*
3 September 2005

Just occasionally in my life, I have been forced to look at my garden in a totally different way. To look at it not as a haven and sanctuary of tranquillity and beauty, but as somewhere foreign, mysterious and potentially dangerous. The last time I did this was when my two children were very small and just beginning to explore the world beyond the nursery, when charming rustic stone steps suddenly became obstacles of potential injury, plants took on a very sinister cast and gardening was an activity carved up into fractions of minutes, rather than hours, between anxious glances and lunges at destructive, self-forgetful toddlers. Despite the wearing watchfulness, precious flowers were picked and discarded, flower bulbs eaten and, most infuriatingly for a gardening journalist, vital labels deliberately misplaced. This stage seemed to last for ever, although it was probably no more than four or five seasons in all. Then gradually things went back to normal as the children learnt some sense and respect, and incidents became confined to cricket balls slicing off dahlia heads, or a trail of heavy footprints in a border. I breathed again and slowly went back to being a proper gardener once more.

Now, I find myself in something of the same position once more, having acquired a young Clumber spaniel puppy of great charm but little sense, for whom my garden is a wonderland of sights, smells and, most particularly, tastes. Because of the need to housetrain him quickly, I spend much of the day standing on the lawn, while he launches himself at remarkable speed into the borders, picking up stones or snails or plucking leaves as he goes. In the years since my children were small, I have planted a tranche of toxic plants – euphorbias, yew and rue, for example – and he goes at them with the unerring instinct of a drunk making his way once more to the bar. (Clumber spaniels have form for this kind of behaviour, in my experience. We once owned one who would pick the daffodils in spring, nipping them off near the base so neatly that I could put them in a vase.)

But what he likes most of all is to roll in the ground-cover *Acaena*, covering himself in hooked burrs in the process. These burrs demonstrate the sophistication of evolved seed-dispersal mechanisms but are immensely tiresome to remove from a spaniel's coat.

I remain resolutely cheerful about all this present mayhem, however, for it seems to me that, from time to time, it does gardeners good to look at aspects of the garden which normally pass them by. I have reacquainted myself intimately with the shape of the hornbeam leaf, for example, since the puppy has taken to snatching at extended stems of the hedge, which protects the fruit trees in the orchard. And I have learned to see more clearly the beauty of arching grasses, such as *Stipa*, not just for their aesthetic qualities but as leaping targets for athletic spaniels. And, if I tire of all this, I can console myself with the thought that, with a puppy, this process of learning through play will soon be over, and I should be left with a sober(ish) and well-behaved adult dog. It may be toddlerdom, but thankfully played out in fast motion.

10

'Borderlines', *Daily Telegraph*
5 January 2008

It is remarkable what a cold December will do to the psyche. The days of sub-zero temperatures and very sharp night frosts worked on me like a tonic. I revelled in the deep pink sunsets and the clear night skies, and marvelled at the beauty of the rimey garden grasses and frosted lawns. (No one in the family was allowed to walk across these, for fear of both burning the grass and spoiling the pristine nature of the ice crystals, so they were forced to tip-toe single-file round them along the thin brick mowing edge.)

So used have I become to mild Decembers that, when the weather became seriously cold in the middle of the month, only the dahlias had already been tucked up snugly beneath a warm blanket of leaf mould. Everything else frost-tender was waiting for me to find a succession of idle moments after Christmas, and they suffered as a result. In particular, the leaves of eucomis and other late-flowering bulbs planted in a sheltered, south-facing border were frozen to a dark-green, slimy mush. In the greenhouse, the untimely breakdown of the heater spelled the death of a banana plant and a vireya rhododendron, and a decidedly sick reaction from streptocarpus and citrus.

Nothing, however, could puncture my bullish mood. I viewed the stubby little *Galanthus elwesii* leaves poking through the ground, some three weeks later than last year, as a good sign. Suddenly, it seemed that we might be returning to more conventional and reassuring climatic times, when winter started in late November, and rarely loosened its grip until early March; when frosted plants were one of the commonplace hazards of gardening. It occurred to me that it was some years since I had said the words 'I think I may have lost that plant from frost.' How good it sounded!

My reaction is irrational and delusional, of course, but there are two genuine reasons to be cheerful. The first is that we gardeners need an excuse to replace plants. Only the most ruthless (and successful, it must be said) will dig up and throw away healthy plants, in order to make room for something new and interesting. Sometimes, the rest of us need the weather to decide the issue for us.

The second is that, although I am pleased that I now feel confident about experimenting with frost-hardy plants (that is ones that cannot withstand temperatures below 23°F/–5°C), I have been badly shaken by recent extreme weather incidents. Evidence is emerging of the disastrous effects last year's weather – the hot early spring and the weeks upon weeks in summer of (often) torrential rain – has had on our wild creatures, in particular their ability to raise progeny successfully. Everything from tiny insects, bees and butterflies to birds and small mammals has been badly affected. Having spent so much time and thought fostering these creatures, I find this dispiriting and anxious. Any reversion, however temporary, to the weather that we still think of as the norm – that is what we knew twenty years ago – is therefore balm to the soul. That is why, should the ceanothus and cistus slowly die next spring, I shall be the last to complain about it, or begrudge the money spent on replacements.

'Borderlines', *Daily Telegraph*
12 February 2005

Gardeners spend a great deal of time thinking and talking about the climate in general and the weather in particular. Or if they don't, they jolly well should, because these things govern our activities. The climate has demonstrably altered, even in my short lifetime.

Instead of worrying about wrapping frost-tender plants like dummies in sacking in November, or knocking snow off the branches of evergreens, they should be much more concerned about sheltering hedges from windburn while making plans to prevent the terrace flooding after torrential summer downpours. As for weeding – it's now a year-round job.

I have a reference book called *The Gardening Year*, published in 1979. I used to use it to jog my memory about arcane operations, such as bud-notching and bridge-grafting, or to tell me when to carry out common tasks such as sowing spring cabbage and picking apple varieties, to make sure I didn't miss the moment.

These days, however, the book languishes on the shelf; its information on timings is no longer completely reliable. In the past decade, in particular, I have made my own timetables based on my experience in this garden.

When, twenty-five years ago and newly married, I moved to east Northamptonshire, I was delighted by almost everything I saw. The rolling green countryside, the seemly cottages, the ancient market towns, the fine medieval churches and grand country houses, and the gruff kindliness of Midlanders all seemed enchanting. I felt like the naïve heroine of a Victorian novel, determined to delight in each new circumstance. But even my heart, young and optimistic as it was, sank at the thought of the climate. While friends of mine found cushy gardening jobs in warm and wet Devon, or sunny Sussex, I would have to struggle for ever (or so I thought) with a cold, dry, windy climate – enough to wither every ceanothus and abutilon that I might want to plant. Winter would be dreary, with little colour.

These past few winters, however, I feel as if my garden has been transported about a hundred miles to the south and west. The indicator plant is *Viburnum* × *bodnantense* 'Dawn', which always flowered freely in the south, yet here would be halted in its tracks in February by hard frosts, which reached deep into the ground and lasted for weeks. No longer. This year, its delicious, pink, honey-and-almond scented flowers have not suffered a moment's setback.

Frosts have melted in the morning, and the only sprinkling of snow lasted just a couple of hours. The cost of heating the greenhouse has fallen, which has encouraged me to be more adventurous about what I grow in it.

We are not through the winter yet, of course, and my hubris may call forth a terrible nemesis, which would serve me right. But I must say that it now looks as if I can have all the advantages of living in the Midlands while enjoying a climate more reminiscent of the south.

* *This article cannot be said to be consistent with the one before, but a gal can change her mind....*

Daily Telegraph
17 February 2007

Climate change? We gardeners have been adjusting to the changing circumstances brought on by changing weather patterns for years. I don't know about you, but I rarely consult the books I bought when I first became a gardener; they describe a landscape I just don't recognize any more. I feel like an explorer in uncharted territory, at once excited and full of trepidation. I live in the Midlands, not Cornwall, yet I am facing the possibility that this winter I shall see very few, if any, hard frosts – that is below 23°F/–5°C – and at the same time there will be a good number of days when the temperature exceeds 50°F/10°C.

Of course, that is not entirely a good thing as far as the effects on the physiology of plants are concerned. Hardy woody plants have a 'winter chill' requirement – that is, they need to experience so many 'hours' (actually, 'chill units') when the temperature is below 45°F/7°C, to ensure that they break dormancy and initiate bud break at the end of winter. Horticulturists worry that the winter chill requirements of some fruits may not be met, in future years, in the south of England, leading to sparse or poor-quality blossom. Blackcurrants, in particular, are under threat, if winters continue to get warmer, together with some apple and raspberry cultivars. Beech trees have a high chill requirement so may leaf later in spring. Fortunately, the dormancy of herbaceous perennials is mostly governed by day length, so they will continue to start growing at the same time as before.

Those plants, for example hawthorn, that have a low chill requirement are brought into leaf earlier than we consider the norm after warm winters. Although the incidence and severity of late spring frosts has declined markedly since the 1970s, so the scientists say, the risk of damage done by any there are increases in those circumstances. Tender young foliage and blossom can be blasted by warming up too quickly in the bright sunshine, which so often follows a cold night, when pressure is high. Even shrubs generally considered hardy, such as hydrangeas, can be knocked back hard. Thin-skinned trees, such as acers, may suffer bark splitting. We must be careful what we plant in east-facing sites, in particular, and be prepared to prune out dieback in early summer.

On the upside, the growing season is three weeks longer now than it was fifty years ago. Shorter winters and sunnier, frost-free autumns give non-native fruits the opportunity to mature properly. Nurserymen are on to this: it is commonplace now to find a range of selected dessert grapes ('Regent', 'Gagarin Blue' and 'Phoenix', for example) offered in fruit catalogues, as well as new apricot cultivars, like 'Tomcot', which give northern gardeners the opportunity, if they have a sheltered, sunny wall, to try these delectable fruits. The Agroforestry Research Trust sells French and Italian cultivars of olive, for both table and culinary use. There has been a report of bananas ripening outside in Cornwall. Some non-native vegetables can also prosper: there is, for example, a purple-sprouting broccoli, 'Bordeaux' F1, which, if sown in February, can be harvested in the late summer, since it does not require winter chilling to initiate its flower buds.

The truth is that we can increasingly experiment with traditional notions of plant hardiness. We need not necessarily be deterred if the plant encyclopaedia rates a plant 'frost-hardy', meaning only hardy down to 23°F/–5°C. There may be no period this winter when temperatures go below that, so why shy away from glorious shrubs like *Ceanothus impressus*, *Mahonia lomariifolia*, *Edgeworthia chrysantha* or *Abutilon vitifolium* or 'Ashford Red'? For northern gardeners, so often treated to pictures of beautiful plants in newspapers and magazines and then told firmly that they can't grow them – destined, like Tantalus, to long for fruits growing just beyond his grasp – there is reason to cheer. (It must be said, that if we become more adventurous, we do have to make sure that soil drainage is good; that is because a warm and wet winter, such as we are experiencing, is a combination designed to encourage fungal diseases which attack roots, in particular *Phytophthora cinnamomi*.)

Then there are all those frost-tender perennials, like dahlias, *Salvia patens* and cannas, whose top-growth dies down in the winter, but which survive, because there is no cold weather prolonged enough to freeze the roots in the soil. If you remember to put a thick dry mulch on your borders in the autumn, as well as the spring, a whole range of frost-tender plants will survive from year to year, without the fiddle-faddle of digging them up and storing them.

An adventurous spirit is not without its dangers, of course. You risk dead plants, frosted blossom, no fruit, wasted money and other disappointments. But the rewards, if they come, will be sweet. As Erasmus Darwin put it: 'A fool is a man who never tried an experiment in his life.' Frankly, I would rather be thought foolhardy than a fool.

The Spectator
21 April 2007

Time was when golden mimosa was an exotic plant you bought in a florist in January, or admired when on a winter holiday in the south of France or Cornwall. No longer. The little puffy balls of yellow flowers are moving north and east. The Mimosa Meter registers *Acacia dealbata* in London and in sheltered gardens all the way up to north Humberside. Since it will tolerate a few degrees of frost for short periods, it might be now worth planting anywhere in the lowlands of England and Wales. That is, if this last winter is part of a pattern, as the scientists tell us it is, rather than an aberration.

Changing climate, we are told, means stronger winds, particularly in autumn and spring, together with wet, mild winters that produce only the odd, short-lived episode of snow and no sustained periods of freezing weather, less incidence of spring frosts and then long, hot, dry summers. When we gardeners first had an inkling of change some thirty years ago (the summer of 1976, remember?), we rubbed our hands because it meant both that we could enjoy longer, hotter summers outside and that we could grow non-native plants which previously we had considered too frost-tender to survive outside. It is only in recent years that the downside – trees blowing over in terrifying gales, flooded gardens, water shortages in summer, lack of winter chilling for dormant fruit trees and bushes, excessive weed growth – has been forcibly borne in on us. We have not been careful enough about what we wished for.

Take historic gardens, for example, especially those maintained by the National Trust and English Heritage as examples of particular design traditions. What a shock it was when trees at Petworth, planted by Capability Brown and painted by J.M.W. Turner, were blown over on 16 October 1987. But, in recent years, it has been summer drought which has done almost as much harm, promoting pest attack and rot in important trees in gardens, while excessive rain in winter has encouraged box blight and thus ruined many a knot garden. Damage to historic gardens adversely affects not only our garden heritage, of course, but also tourism and employment, especially in the countryside.

Most gardens are not historic, or the preserved vision of a particular gardener, of course, so for many gardeners rising temperatures and, in particular, lack of winter frosts seem to promise the opportunity to plunder the floras of the sub-tropics. Agaves, cannas, bananas and tree ferns can now be grown all year round in London and warm, sheltered places in the south and south-west. If you want to see what is possible already, visit Tresco Abbey Gardens in the Scilly Isles, where temperatures rarely go below 50°F/10°C, or Cotswold Wildlife Park in Oxfordshire, where the walled garden no longer contains vegetables but, instead, meerkats cosily ensconced amongst agaves, opuntias, puyas and dasylirions.

These are very particular instances and, if it had not been for the late Christopher Lloyd, might perhaps have remained so – for a while at least. Lloyd's grubbing up of his rose garden (fair enough) at Great Dixter in East Sussex and the planting of the space with sub-tropical plants had a seismic effect on gardeners. Without his imprimatur, I suspect that far fewer gardeners would have felt tempted to follow suit, since sub-tropical plants powerfully change the look of a garden.

Personally, I don't want my garden to look like a hotel garden in Majorca; I find the clashing pinks and oranges tire the eye and, even in these changed times, the strength of light in this country rarely mitigates entirely the garishness. Moreover, these plantings hardly suit our varied regional vernacular house styles, of which we are so justifiably proud. It is not just a dislike for the unfamiliar: it is that the scale seems wrong. Many sub-tropical plants have very large leaves and strident colours; they are imposing, impressive and exotic. This is a problem particularly in the countryside, where context should be so important. Purple-leaved banana plants are even more foreign than the yellow-leaved conifers that so many village dwellers think appropriate.

A more sympathetic approach, to my mind, is to use plants from a Mediterranean climate (those not only from southern Europe bordering the inland sea, but also from the Cape in South Africa, Chile, south-western Australia and California), many of which struggled to survive harsh winters in the past. Sensitivity needs to be employed with these as well, but plants like cistuses, lavenders and shrubby salvias are old friends and climate change gives us the opportunity to grow the more tender members of genera we already grow. It makes sense to scour the books and catalogues for 'borderline hardy' plants from Mediterranean regions.

The change in climate is likely to be viewed with most satisfaction in the north of England and Scotland – where gardeners deserve a bit of a break, let's face it. The most northerly vineyard used to be at Renishaw in Derbyshire; now it is at Carnforth in Lancashire. Figs ripen in north Yorkshire, apricots are grown commercially in Cambridgeshire. Since summers are getting longer, trees from southern Europe, originally, such as the common walnut, may well be now worth planting north of York. If I were a garden-minded City gent with a bonus burning a hole in my pocket, I would extend my search for a country estate beyond Devon, Somerset and Gloucestershire and think of Staffordshire, Worcestershire, Monmouthshire, Derbyshire or Lancashire as well.

We have to ask what happens, in these changed circumstances, to existing gardens and plantings, based very largely on reliably frost-hardy trees, shrubs, herbaceous perennials and bulbs; the kind of gardens for which we are particularly known across the world, and in which a number of discrete styles have been developed over the last four hundred years.

It seems to me that there are a number of relatively easy things we can do to mitigate the worst effects of climate change on them. We should plant everything small, especially trees, so that they are well anchored by an extensive root system in the soil and able to withstand gales. We should lighten heavy soils with grit and bark chippings, so that plant roots are not sitting in sopping soil through the winter. For those plants which need moisture in summer, such as some South African bulbs, we should mulch the soil heftily in spring, so that it stays moist despite a beating sun in July; in the case of frost-tender plants, the mulching should be done in the autumn to prevent the roots from freezing. We should plant shelter belts and, if that interferes with the view, then internal shelters using hedging plants. Northern European perennials, which need substantial winter chilling, should be planted in the coldest part of the garden, if possible.

You may wonder whether it is worth that bother, to maintain our hold on traditional types of garden making, using well-tried plants, with which we have become comfortable. The alternative, however, is to risk a mish-mash of conflicting styles. Just because we *can* get something to grow does not mean we *have* to. For myself, I shall refrain from planting a mimosa yet awhile.

'Borderlines', *Daily Telegraph*
28 August 2004

This is a tale of the unexpected. On the evening of the 9th and the morning of the 10th of August, 3.79 inches/96 millimetres of rain fell on our village, 2 inches/50 millimetres in a single hour,* a remarkable event for this region and time of year, and one with baleful consequences. The street became a fast-flowing river, cars were abandoned and people had to wade home with their trousers rolled up. Much of the water had run off the fields behind the village, a summer-dry heavy clay which could not possibly absorb such a deluge. Despite determined efforts by villagers and firemen, several houses were flooded. Concerned neighbours, sheltering under huge colourful umbrellas that gave them a falsely festive air, met to commiserate and to help those badly affected. Although not in the Boscastle class of disaster, it was nevertheless a crisis keenly felt by everyone in this close-knit community. Only the children enjoyed the novelty, biking through the floods or standing under the arcing sprays of water pumped away by the firemen.

In our garden, we watched with anxiety as the water flooded the orchard, the fruit cage, the greenhouses, several flower beds and the terrace at the back of the house. We were forced to place sandbags in front of the French windows, as the flood threatened to inundate the house. In one place on the terrace, there was 6 inches/150 millimetres of standing water. Onions, tomatoes and roses growing close to a paved path were partly submerged for three days. Eventually, the water receded, although as I write the threat is by no means over, since the weather is still unsettled and the surrounding fields at saturation point.

Everyone agrees that waterlogging is bad for plants. To begin with, standing water suffocates roots and encourages the growth of fungal diseases such as forms of *Phytophthora*. Neither of these undesirables become evident immediately; indeed, if a tree dies next spring I may not necessarily immediately twig that it was the August 2004 floods that did for it. Even if plants do not die, the high humidity will foster blights, bacterial leaf spots and botrytis of almost biblical plague proportions.

Some damage is already evident. The leaves of the once-submerged tomatoes are browning and I know my onions won't keep, even when finally dried off. As for annuals and perennials, I have cut back damaged or yellowing ground-hugging leaves and sprayed the plants with a foliar feed to try to stimulate new roots to grow, but the tobacco plants look as sick as I feel, and a variegated sage is wilting and will die.

I am conscious that we gardeners may have opened ourselves up more to the possibility of flooding in recent years. The fashion for large areas of paving, especially if concreted rather than laid on sand beds, makes it harder for heavy rain to drain away quickly. When we moved here, the lawn came practically up to the back door; now we have an extensive and, I see, water-retaining terrace.

The flooding put into doubt the projected gardens opening on Bank Holiday Monday. This is a proven raiser of substantial funds for the church, and good fun, but gardens were looking distinctly battered and sodden, and one had been substantially damaged. In the end, we resolved that it should be 'business as usual', even if fewer gardens than usual were open. And I have resolved that, in future, I won't take our generally low rainfall for granted, but always expect the unexpected instead.

*I am indebted to Geoff, who lives round the corner and has sophisticated measuring equipment, for this information.

The Spectator
September 2005

All my working life, I have been adapting to climate change. As an apprentice in a garden near Antwerp in the summer of 1976, I spent the early mornings and evenings (we could not work in the day, since the temperatures topped 104°F/40°C) trying to save the languishing, but famous, collection of rhododendrons, by watering them from dustbins filled at a borehole. That early experience gave me both a sharper eye for stress in plants and a scepticism about the immutability of circumstances.

I don't appear to be unusual. In recent years, in our best private and public gardens, there has been much adventurous experimenting, both with plants that will withstand high temperatures and summer droughts, and with the soil conditions that suit them.

At the same time, interested public bodies have been sponsoring and commissioning research, publishing findings and holding conferences, in an attempt to get us gardeners to understand the implications of climate change for our gardens. There is, for example, *Gardening in the Global Greenhouse: Climate Change in Gardens*, a useful, if scarifying, report from the University of Reading (2002), and also the findings of a conference on the impact of climate change on British trees, held at the University of Surrey in June (both reports may be found on www.rhs.org.uk).

The main thrust of these is that we can expect higher temperatures and more frequent droughts in summer and shorter, milder, wetter winters, as well as torrential rain leading to flash floods in summer, stronger winds and more storms. A rise in temperatures will help foreign pests establish themselves, in places where they may have no natural predators. Those already established will do better and move further north, and fungal diseases such as powdery mildews and honey fungus are likely to get worse. Most weeds won't suffer; quite the reverse, since those seed bearers like groundsel will cram in more generations a year. Lawns will be harder to maintain in conventional ways.

There will be an effect on both native and exotic trees. The competitive balance between species will change, with beech trees in particular suffering in the south, and sycamore and holm oaks probably benefiting. As for tree and soft fruit, the requirement by apple and pear trees for a period of winter 'chilling' may put them under pressure, as blackcurrants already are.

As for soils, the effect of soil warming will be complex, but, undoubtedly, organic matter will break down faster and we are likely to get increased plant growth in the short term, although there will be a loss of soil nitrogen eventually. Soil carbon will be lost more quickly by oxidation, a crucial concern on, for example, peaty soils.

But, and it is an important but, there will be plenty of benign consequences: quicker seed germination and growth rates, lower glasshouse heating bills, a wider choice of exotic plants and better ripening of non-native fruits because of longer growing seasons. Northern gardeners can become more adventurous. After all, a crisping astilbe in Surrey may well mean a ripening apricot in Tweeddale.

Already, gardeners actively seek out those plants they know to be tolerant of drought and drying winds: sub-shrubs from the Mediterranean region or New Zealand, as well as summer- and autumn- flowering bulbs, and prairie perennials. And milder winters have made once borderline tender plants, even sub-tropical ones, such as palms and bananas, possible and popular, especially in sheltered city gardens and those by the sea. Meadow gardening is now a considered alternative to the manicured lawn.

Trees are a problem. Anyone with sense already avoids poplar and willow on shrinkable clay soils, but their thirstiness will put them under stress elsewhere as well. And southern gardeners may find they have to eschew beech for hedging. Let them plant hornbeam, I say. Above all, we must plant trees when small. Bare-rooted 'whips' establish themselves quickest and best, since there is no top-hamper to support and no peaty compost to grow out from, and they are much less likely to suffer from 'wind-blow' in storms.

As for soils, the approach has to be two-pronged: ensuring that they are free draining, by incorporating organic matter or grit on heavy soils, since waterlogging in wet winters can be fatal to the roots of many plants, and then mulching in spring to prevent the baleful effects of summer drought and to inhibit competing weeds. Organic mulches will also slow the leaching of nutrients from the soil after summer deluges.

Sprinklers need to replaced by seep hoses or trickle irrigation systems, since these provide water at soil level directly to the roots, so much less is lost through evaporation. Water-retaining polyacrylamides should be added to container composts or (shock, horror) containers abandoned altogether. And 'hard' features, like patios, need to be kept small, to lessen the risk of garden (and house) flooding.

The situation is so complex, and often apparently contradictory, that gardeners can only observe their gardens closely and respond, if need be by abandoning traditional practices and garden styles. We private gardeners are luckier, after all, than those who have the care of 'heritage gardens', which are founded on a particular style. Adapting may be tough, for gardeners in the south in particular, but it is better than closing our eyes, putting our hands to our heads and screaming. As for northern gardeners, they can be forgiven a secret, apologetic, smile.

The Spectator
December 2003

A week ago last Saturday, 23 November, at ten o'clock in the morning, I was standing in a wood in Northamptonshire, prey to a succession of dreadful anxieties. I was 'picking up' on a shoot and waiting, with an excited yellow Labrador, for a drive to begin. But my thoughts were elsewhere – partly at home, and partly half a world away. One tranche of anxieties you will have guessed already: would Steve Thompson find his jumpers, would Matt Dawson give fatal lip to the referee, was Mike Tindall a better bet than Mike Catt, could Stirling Mortlock, George Smith and Lote Tuqiri really be neutralized?* England might be the better side, but how could you ever count out a country whose very personality seems defined by Steve Waugh? On and on they went, one worry chasing another, like clouds scudding across a stormy sky.

The other anxieties concerned my garden. A few days earlier, I had planted tulip bulbs into ground completely dry 2 inches/5 centimetres below the surface. So dry, in fact, that I had had to water the planting holes first before putting in the bulbs, a unique experience in mid-November, in my gardening lifetime at least.

This is the legacy of such a dry and hot season, of course. Between 1 March and 18 November, a mere 10.5 inches/262.5 millimetres of rain fell on my garden, much of it useless to plant life, because the strong summer sun almost immediately evaporated it. In the same period, the year before, when summer temperatures were lower, mind, the figure was 19.7 inches/492.5 millimetres. Now that was a good growing year.

If the shortfall was not made up this winter, I worried, the effect, particularly on deciduous trees and shrubs, in the spring, would be serious indeed. They would come into growth, but there would be little moisture for the roots to draw on, yet they would still be losing water vapour heavily from the new leaves. Since plant nutrients must be dissolved before they can be taken up, not only would these woody plants thirst, but they would hunger as well. Already, I knew I had to prepare myself for a disappointing spring for daffodils. They make their flower buds the autumn before and come up 'blind' if the soil is dry then. It was too late now to save them from that.

I have a clay soil, the worst sort in a drought, and the water table is too low for capillary action to work to the benefit of the upper levels of the soil. When water is scarce, surface tension holds what there is more tightly to clay particles than any other kind, making it unavailable to plant roots. Moreover, water percolates only very slowly, so what rain does fall takes a long time to make its way through.

Water, the most basic of all life-giving commodities, creates atavistic fears when it seems to fail or fall short. A few weeks before, I had seen a newspaper photograph of the ruins of Mardale, the village flooded to make Haweswater reservoir in Cumbria in the 1930s, emerging out of the water once more. This struck fear into my heart – not to mention, presumably, the hearts of all those Mancunians who depend on it when brushing their teeth.

As I stood in the wood, I tried to compute how much rain would have to fall in the next three months, in order to ensure that the trees in my garden would not be put under severe pressure in the spring. I had invested too much emotional and other capital in my 'wood'; after ten years, the trees should have been safe from drought, yet I feared they were not. At a rough guess, we needed at least 120 per cent of our usual winter rainfall, I decided, before the beginning of March – that is about 13 inches/330 millimetres. Last winter, admittedly considered a very dry one, only 8 inches/203 millimetres fell here.

Mercifully, there was one settler of nerves, that morning. It was raining – steadily, vertically, out of a calm but leaden sky. And, as the cold water trickled down my neck, splashed off my waterproofs and froze my hands, my heart lightened and my spirits rose. This was the start of the rain, surely, that might just save my trees from disaster.

And so it turned out. By the end of the day, almost an inch/25 millimetres had fallen, with no sun to evaporate it or prevent its gradual percolation through the layers of soil. And the forecast was for more the next day, and the next week. Indeed, by the following Sunday, nearly 2 inches/50 millimetres had fallen. Eleven to go. Long before that, however, I knew the result from the Telstra Stadium. So, no worries, mate – as the Aussies say – or not until the Six Nations in February, at least.

It was the day of the Rugby Union World Cup Final between England and Australia – how could we forget?

11

 TAME AND WILD CREATURES

'Borderlines', *Daily Telegraph*
24 November 2007

My husband has an ancient, much-washed T-shirt, which bears the legend: 'Whereinthehellis Madison, Ohio?' In fact, he and I know perfectly well where the hell it is, since we have a good friend, Tim Brotzman, who lives in this village on the southern shore of Lake Erie. He is a respected tree and shrub nurseryman of considerable skill and tremendous work ethic, who gave my husband the garment when we were staying with him one summer. It is not the only present he has given, as a matter of fact, for I own a spade, which bears another legend: 'A.M Leonard and Son, Piqua, Ohio. Heat Treated'. Kindly, enthusiastic Tim brought it over one year, carefully wrapped, in his luggage. Whenever I use it, I am reminded of happy student days at the Royal Horticultural Society garden at Wisley in 1975, when we spent prodigious amounts of time double-digging. Tim is tall and powerful, as befits a nurseryman, and this spade has a blade as square and honed as his beard.

You may think that this is all very nice for me, but what possible relevance might it have for British gardening? Well, none quite yet, but it shortly will. In 1991, Tim was told of a unique weeping form of *Cercis canadensis*, which the Americans call the eastern redbud, in the garden of a Miss Connie Covey in Westfield, New York. Miss Covey had lived with her mother, and the story which Tim managed gently to elicit from her was that her mother found this tree at a 'rest stop' whilst on a journey home from Florida, some thirty-five years before. By the time Tim saw it, it had reached 4 feet 5 inches/1.3 metres tall by 7 feet/2.1 metres wide, with a trunk diameter of 6 inches/15 centimetres. The stems are gently twisted and the habit compact. The heart-shaped leaves are dark green, slightly larger than the normal species and held so that they look as if they are 'shingled', like overlapping tiles. The clusters of lavender flowers are held on the bare branches in spring, and the leaves turn yellow in autumn. It is extremely hardy. Tim bought the rights to propagate and patent this plant, called 'Covey', registering it, for marketing purposes, as 'Lavender Twist'.

From time to time, Tim has sent me details of this tree, and I will shortly receive one to trial in my garden, which is exciting. This plant is already beginning to create a stir, and win awards, in Europe, including a gold medal for the best new plant introduction at Glee (the garden and leisure exhibition) in September. This tree will be widely available from early next April in garden centres, and will be launched officially on to the European market on the Notcutts stand at the Chelsea Flower Show next May.

Nor is this all. Tim has introduced a number of quality plants to the American market, and one or two of them, such as *Hamamelis* 'Orange Encore' and *Cornus kousa* 'Temple Jewel', are beginning to find their way over here. For the last ten years, he has been working to develop a good white-flowered form of the weeping redbud, a project which is coming to fulfilment. With a bit of luck, as time goes on, more and more gardeners will know the answer to the question emblazoned on that T-shirt.

The Spectator
February 2006

Christopher Lloyd died on 27 January. Not since the deaths of Gertrude Jekyll in 1932, William Robinson in 1935 and Vita Sackville-West in 1962 has so much homage been paid in the broadsheets to the memory of a gardener. In the nation at large, more people mourned the deaths of Percy Thrower and Geoff Hamilton, but these were television personalities. Christopher's reputation rested on a weekly column, 'In My Garden', in *Country Life* from 1963 until shortly before his death, his contributions to the *Observer* and the *Guardian*, a succession of thoughtful, opinionated books, such as *The Well-Tempered Garden*, and, most particularly, on his garden and nursery at Great Dixter in East Sussex, a draw for garden enthusiasts for almost fifty years.

He was lucky with his situation. His parents, Nathaniel and Daisy Lloyd, bought the fifteenth-century manor house in 1910. Edwin Lutyens, a friend, remodelled it and added a hall house of the same age, which had been taken to bits and brought the 4 miles from Benenden. Lutyens, with Nathaniel, laid out the garden in strongly geometrical fashion, incorporating tidied-up out-buildings, and employing pleasing detailing, for which Lutyens was famous, such as tiles on edge in paving and arches. Several formal gardens, enclosed by evergreen hedging, were laid out around the house. Nathaniel Lloyd continued the Arts and Crafts tradition by putting in a sunk garden with octagonal pool, as well as masses of quirky topiary. He even wrote a book, *Garden Craftsmanship in Yew and Box*, on the subject.

The Arts and Crafts atmosphere of the garden explains much of the enduring popularity and importance of this garden, since it is a style to which we gardeners instinctively cleave. Indeed, its popularity was an important reason why Modernist gardens in the 1930s failed to make any impact on the collective psyche of garden owners. Why bother with concrete, glass and grass when you could have finely turned vernacular details and formal enclosures, which you could then fill to bursting with flowers? Christopher Lloyd's contribution to the fashioning of gardens since the war has been constantly to reassure gardeners that this kind of gardening was worth aspiring to. He never stopped experimenting with plants and their associations, but within a garden layout which is nearly a century old.

Influenced by both Robinson and Jekyll (he met the latter as a small boy) his great strengths were his acute powers of observation and a fascination with plants, their form, their function, their clubbability, as well as an adventurous spirit in the placing of them. He understood the importance of providing succession; this is the really difficult trick to pull off, as any gardener will tell you, but vital in contemporary gardens, most of which are too small for comfort. There are few people, alive or dead, who knew more about the ways of the plants, which he used with such *brio* in the Long Border, the Exotic Garden (after he had turfed out the roses from Lutyens' Rose Garden) and the 'meadows' which surround and encroach upon the garden.

Christopher always paid handsome tribute to the influence of his mother, Daisy, with whom he lived at Dixter until her death in 1972. She made a 'meadow' out of the drained portion of the moat, as well as planting masses of bulbs, foreign and native, in the rough grass on each side of the path that leads to the house's front porch. Over the years, the management of the meadows has been refined, and Mary Keen, the garden designer and a good friend of Christopher's, believes that meadow gardening is one of his most important legacies. In old age, he even took off to Minnesota to see how prairies looked, coming back to make his own 'prairie' using North American plants. One of the most appealing garden scenes at Dixter is the endlessly thought-about and carefully maintained Long Border divided by only a York-stone-flagged path from the Orchard, with its lax, waving grasses.

Epater le bourgeois was always a game Christopher enjoyed playing, and he and his brilliant friend and head gardener, Fergus Garrett, had tremendous fun in the last ten years with the Exotic Garden, combining the most vibrant colours, using mainly sub-tropical plants, and alarming respectable middle-aged ladies, who came to Dixter in droves. But it was comparatively gentle teasing, really. The Topiary Lawn, which his father used for golf putting practice, is now a meadow, but the clipped topiary shapes remain. Christopher Lloyd taught us that we don't necessarily have to do things very differently – just better, and with all our heart.

I first met Valerie Finnis (1924–2006) when I was about eleven or twelve years old. She had been at the Kerry School, Reigate, with my mother, and a mutual friend had reintroduced them many years later. We only lived a few miles away from Wheatley, where she lived, so she would come and visit, bringing with her little clay pots of alpines, which she called 'treasures', for my sister and me. These, I am afraid, we soon lost from shameful neglect. She certainly seemed one of the more exotic and child-friendly of my mother's friends, at a time when children were mostly politely ignored. When my sister, aged twelve, was in hospital after an accident, Valerie brought her an exquisite little alpine garden on a tray.

Three years later, when my mother died, Valerie came to the funeral (I hardly ever knew her to attend funerals in later life) and made a point of staying in touch thereafter. One day in 1970, we received a card saying that she had married a man called Sir David Scott and had moved to Northamptonshire. She enclosed a picture of them together in the garden. We teenagers thought he looked absolutely ancient (he was, in fact, an extremely sprightly eighty-three, while she was forty-five) and it was a matter of some wonder, since we had no idea that they had met two years before at the Waterperry School of Horticulture, while she was running the alpine department there.

The following year I went up to Cambridge and, from time to time, Valerie would invite me over to spend weekends in the wing of Boughton House (the Duke of Buccleuch's Northamptonshire seat), which had once been the laundry and was later named the Dower House. Here David had lived since 1947, when he retired from the Foreign Office, and had made, with his first wife (who died in 1965), a beautiful, informal garden of trees and shrubs mainly, full of fascination. I loved it there. The house was rambling, old-fashioned and agreeably shabby, since it had not been 'done up' since Edwardian times, when David's father, an admiral in the navy, had lived there with his family when on leave. There were, puzzlingly, *two* basins in the downstairs loo. The drawing-room had a huge fireplace, on which whole logs simmered, and on the right-hand side of which David habitually sat in a winged chair. I slept in the Butterfly Room upstairs, whose walls were hung with wonderful watercolours of New Guinea butterflies, painted by David's extremely talented Australian aunt, Ellis Rowan, and later sold by Valerie in aid of the Merlin Trust. The days were spent in the garden, weeding and pruning; the tool handles were all painted white so that they could be retrieved easily, once put down.

Both Valerie and David spent all the daylight hours in the garden, in good weather and bad, always accompanied by a pug dog. The atmosphere was of serious-minded endeavour, in which guests were expected to join, but enlivened with jokes and 'tea-tea' stops, when we would sit in the summerhouse eating cake and drinking tea out of thermoses. They were old-school gardeners, who believed, like Kipling, that half a proper gardener's work is done upon his knees. Every piece of couch grass was meticulously removed by hand when a new bed was made.

You never quite knew who you might meet at the Dower House: Joan Hassall, the woodcut engraver, perhaps, Norman Parkinson, the society photographer, Tony Ireson, the local historian, Princess Margaret if she was staying 'next door' and had asked to see the garden, or Ted Barrett, the erstwhile Irish peat-digger who helped build the raised beds along the walls of David's kitchen garden to accommodate the alpines which arrived from Waterperry after it closed in 1971. While training at Wisley in 1975, I organized a trip of staff (including Ken Aslet and Martyn Rix) and students to the Dower House; it must have been June because the 'Golden Chersonese' rose was flowering fit to bust. I should be surprised if any one of those students has forgotten the welcome, and the fun of it.

One Dower House visitor I met often was Jim Carr (J.L. Carr, the novelist) who lived near by, in Kettering. We were introduced when he came to show David and Valerie a slide show, entitled 'The Hidden Treasures of Northamptonshire'. And he was one of the guests (as were my husband and myself) at the last dinner party held at the Dower House before David died, when Valerie played one of the practical jokes for which she was well known. She employed a young butler and a middle-aged cook for the evening and, while we were sipping sherries, the cook kept appearing from the kitchen, looking more and more cross and flustered and whispering in Valerie's ear. Valerie spoke to her quite sternly, and apologized to us for her behaviour. Eventually, she came back in, took off her apron with a flourish and demanded a drink of the 'butler'. At this point, they were unmasked, as Mrs Anthony Chenevix-Trench and her son, Jonathan, old friends of Valerie's. I shall long remember the look of astonishment on Jim's face.

The great day in the year was the Sunday in summer when the garden was open for the National Gardens Scheme. People came as much as a hundred miles to see this garden, made by two such famous gardeners, and to snap up rarities at the plant sale held at the same time. Along with Martyn Rix, Robin and Joan Grout, Netta Statham and other gardening friends, I used to help to sell plants, and it was a tricky business since you had to be a real alpine expert to recognize some of the plants in their little pots. *Phlox* 'Chattahoochee' always sold out first, I remember. Jim Carr and others were posted in the garden to prevent any stealing of cuttings or plants, about which Valerie felt a morbid horror.

I used to meet them at the Royal Horticultural Society's Vincent Square shows as well, to which they came in Valerie's Morris Minor, with plants to put up for awards, carefully stowed on the back seat. David would sit on the dais in the New Hall, looking on, while Valerie socialized or attended Joint Rock or Floral Committee 'B' meetings. They rarely came away without an Award of Merit or, at the very least, a Cultural Commendation. They were a force for good in the horticultural world, and there are many people still about who have ample reason to be grateful to them.

The Spectator
August 2005

The rose has long been an international symbol of peace and reconciliation. A striking example is 'Peace', which was bred by Meilland in the south of France, was smuggled out to the United States during the last war and became the first rose to be named after the war ended. Another is the Rose Garden in the Park of Peace and Friendship, close to the site of the completely razed village of Lidice, a mining village in the present-day Czech Republic. This park, dedicated in 1955, is a memorial to one of the worst Nazi atrocities of the Second World War when, in June 1942, the village men were shot, their womenfolk sent to Ravensbrück concentration camp, and most of their children despatched to Chełmno, where they were gassed. As most people know, the massacre was carried out as a reprisal for the killing of Reinhard Heydrich, 'the Butcher of Prague', by two Czech agents. Interestingly, the idea for the Rose Garden came originally from the English 'Lidice shall live' Committee, chaired by Dr (later Sir) Barnett Stross, MP, which also raised £37,000 to help rebuild Lidice close to the old site. The rest of the world piled in and nearly 30,000 roses were donated to the park by thirty-five different countries; 7,000 of these came from Harry Wheatcroft's nursery in Nottinghamshire, from where the British effort was coordinated. 'Peace' figured prominently amongst them. (Harry Wheatcroft, as older readers will remember, was a flamboyant bewhiskered rosarian, a lifelong socialist and pacifist, much given to wearing loud suits.) A song, entitled 'A Rose for Lidice', was composed by Alan Rawsthorne soon after. The English connections don't end with Stross or Wheatcroft, however, for the exiled President of Czechoslovakia, Eduard Benes, and his wife spent the war in leafiest Buckinghamshire. They lived at the Abbey, a country house in the picturesque village of Aston Abbotts, near Aylesbury. Churchill would come over to visit from nearby Chequers, and much of the Czech resistance was organized from here, including the fateful planning for the assassination of Heydrich. In October 1943, to mark the twenty-fifth anniversary of the birth of an independent Czechoslovakia (the German invasion notwithstanding), Benes planted a lime tree in the grounds of the Abbey. Limes, being long-lived and stately, are commonly planted in eastern Europe to mark important anniversaries.

The anniversary tree is a fine, 40-foot/12-metre-tall specimen of the European lime (*Tilia* × *europaea*). I viewed it from a nearby grassy field, where once stood the medieval village, now only bumps and hollows in the ground. The tree was pointed out to me by Victor Scott, a naturalist and retired professional gardener who has lived and worked in Aston Abbotts all his life, and who knew the Beneses during the war. As a schoolboy, he learned some Czech so that he could greet them in their own language and, after they left for home in February 1945, Mrs Benes sent Victor a book about her country, signed by her husband. The next year, while on a tour of Europe, Victor knocked on the door of the presidential palace in Prague and was invited in for dinner.

It is a source of great satisfaction to him that the Czech links with Aston Abbotts remain strong and, in particular, since he is a gardener, that flowers are an essential symbol of that. In late April this year, during a long weekend of Anglo-Czech celebrations in Aston to mark the wartime associations as well as the sixtieth anniversary of VE Day, the Czech Ambassador planted a European lime tree on the village green and yellow roses in the churchyard. These were sent from Lidice, propagated from roses growing in the Park of Peace and Friendship. Victor recalls that Wheatcroft named a red Hybrid Tea rose 'Lidice', but it was never in commerce and, sadly, it seems to have died out.

It is easy to forget, if you are deeply immersed in gardening matters as I am, just how important flowers and gardens are in a much broader context, both as symbols and for articulating deep feeling. One only has to consider, for example, poppy wreaths on Remembrance Sunday, white lilies at Easter, and the Commonwealth War Grave cemeteries, which are all gardens of remembrance. We instinctively think of gardens as good, since they are necessarily antithetical to war, strife, bitterness and corruption, while flowers are signs of fresh, unsullied, young life. It is salutary consciously to remember that from time to time.

And it is also salutary, if rather disturbing, to reflect that, if Hitler had won the war, a village which had given refuge to the Czech president in exile, might very well now, like the original Lidice and the medieval village of Aston, be only bumps and hollows in the ground.

The Spectator
December 2006

There are precious few growth areas in horticultural retailing, at the moment, but sales of garden bird food are certainly one of them. Despite the fact that winters are measurably warmer, it seems we gardeners still cannot do too much for our garden birds. Not only do we put out food for them, and hammer nest boxes into every fence and tree, but our approach to gardening in the autumn has also changed. We shiver, like an old lady suspecting a draught, at the thought of cutting down perennials in autumn as our forebears so punctiliously did, lest precious bird-friendly seed heads be lost. We even choose to grow particular plants, such as autumn daisies and late-flowering grasses, almost as much for avian as aesthetic reasons. We have been told many times that the numbers of many birds, both farmland and woodland/garden species, are on the decline and we are determined to help if we can. It is all very admirable, and has had some perceptible beneficial effects. Certain species are thriving, as they have not done for decades. Thirty years ago, a charm of goldfinches (surely the prettiest of all finches with their red faces and broad yellow bars on the black wings) was a rare sight in any garden that I knew. Now, thanks partly to our determination to hang on to thistly seed heads in winter, and partly to our choice of birdseed, they are almost commonplace.

There are a number of disadvantages to feeding birds, of course, which we cannot duck, so to speak. One is that the occupants of bird tables attract sparrowhawks, and there is scarcely a more distressing sight for a householder than a sparrowhawk swooping down and carrying off a small bird. Either bird tables have to be placed right against the house or other solid structure, or we have to accept that sparrowhawks must eat as well. Another is the way bird feeders and tables are magnets to squirrels, creatures with the same toxic mix of charm and malignity as magpies and domestic cats. And, if you go in for bird feeding, it must be done consistently and with regard to hygiene. Presently an outbreak of *Trichomoniasis* is killing finches and house sparrows, and the advice from the British Trust for Ornithology is to disinfect feeding stations and bird baths frequently to inhibit the spread.

A number of bird species are beneficial to gardeners – tits eat aphids, thrushes eat snails and green woodpeckers find ants in lawns, for example – and only pigeons, pheasants and domesticated chickens have the power to do much damage. The depredations of wood pigeons have, however, forced me to give up growing brassicas altogether, since the aesthetic compromises necessary to scare them away – glitterbangs, plastic bags, CDs hanging on strings – cannot be justified, when cabbages are no longer needed to save us from want in winter.

With the exception of annoying collared doves and ruthless magpies, I am happy to see any bird in the garden and I mourn the disappearance from this garden of the spotted flycatcher, which, with the swift, is the most charming of summer visitors. At this time of year, I wait eagerly for the arrival of the migrant fieldfares to eat the last windfalls from under the apple trees, noisy with chatter like a factory canteen. But the bird I really look for is the red kite.

If you have never seen a red kite, I can tell you it has a 5-foot/1.5-metre wingspan, a rufous body, grey head, large white patches on the underside of the wings, black 'fingers' to the wings and a V-shaped tail, which flexes and twists as the bird wheels magisterially in the sky above the garden. It was once a native of the old oakwoods hereabouts but died out in the late nineteenth century; now, after successful re-introduction from Spain, it is breeding naturally and yearly extending its geographical range. Many readers will have experienced the heart-stopping sight of these birds gliding above the M40 in the Chilterns, I dare say. Red kites are mainly scavengers, living off roadkill, myxy rabbits, dead sheep and a few live small mammals. They are sociable birds, who meet together on winter afternoons, like old codgers getting together in the pub. A farmer friend has seen twenty-seven together at one time; my count is a mere, but thrilling, eleven.

So frequently do kites, singly or in pairs, appear above our garden that, last winter, I left out the pluckings of dead pheasants, since I know they need feathers and bones in their diet. However, I gave up when it became plain from the complete disappearance of the leavings each morning that I was only feeding foxes. The red kite can do without me, it seems, but the reverse is certainly not the case.

The Spectator
March 2006

I have been talking tosh. Well, not entirely tosh, but certainly substantial dollops of wishful thinking and airy, groundless supposition, at least. I have come to this conclusion after reading a book by a plant scientist called Ken Thompson. However, it is written in such an engaging, amiable and witty way that my discovery doesn't hurt too much, especially since I can console myself that almost everybody else has been deluded as me.

Ever since Ken Thompson's first book – *An Ear to the Ground: Garden Science for Ordinary Mortals* – was published in 2003, I have been a big fan. He is a senior lecturer in the Department of Animal and Plant Sciences at the University of Sheffield, who left his academic papers briefly to attempt to teach gardeners horticultural science, in a way that they could understand without feeling patronized. As I read it, I could hear the deafening boom and crump of exploding myths. With his second book, *No Nettles Required: The Reassuring Truth about Wildlife Gardening* (Eden Project Books, £10), he is at it again, trying to make us understand garden wildlife and their requirements, using verifiable scientific information. Crump, boom, aaaargh.

Ken Thompson was a key instigator of the first biodiversity survey of urban, private gardens (BUGS), begun in Sheffield in 2000. The aim of this survey was to discover what there really was in the way of wildlife in the average garden – not large rural gardens, where people mostly think the wildlife is, but small or smallish urban gardens, of various ages and gardening regimes. They chose sixty-one, and set up a number of facilities for collecting small wildlife in them, including pitfall traps (for ground-living creatures) and Malaise traps (to capture flying insects).

This project must have been frustrating at times, since money was plainly tight. Sadly, moths were not counted, since the scientists could not depend on anyone getting up before dawn to empty moth traps, and neither were butterflies, since that requires people to run around catching them in nets. Quite often, therefore, Thompson himself bumps up against lack of data, and he is not above the odd airy supposition himself. Nevertheless, BUGS found out a great deal that was not known before, and the results are not only interesting but hugely cheering. In a nutshell, gardens are wildlife havens, often much more plentiful than the (agricultural) countryside. And large gardens are not qualitatively better than small ones.

As well as the data from the BUGS survey, Ken Thompson could draw on the remarkable findings made by Jennifer Owen from 1972, in her suburban garden in Leicester, collated and published as *The Ecology of a Garden: The First Fifteen Years* (Cambridge University Press, 1991). Dr Owen meticulously monitored the wildlife of every kind in her garden over many years and concluded that, over time, more than eight thousand species of insect resided there, together with many other sundry invertebrates, such as millipedes and spiders. This included some species new to science. Of course, we ordinary gardeners haven't a hope of telling a Gasteruptid from an Ichneumon wasp, but it is encouraging to think how rich a world there is, unseen but right under our noses.

Moreover, to promote the interests of wildlife, we apparently need to do little that is onerous. Simply by refusing to use pesticides, particularly insecticides and slug pellets, growing plants with single, nectar-rich flowers as well as trees and shrubs, leaving dead wood around, making compost, not tidying up too much in autumn, digging a pond and letting some grass grow long, we can make a good situation even better. Thompson should earn the gratitude of millions of conscientious wildlife gardeners for telling us that we don't need to grow a nettle patch for butterfly larvae, since nettles are probably Britain's commonest wild plant anyway.

And what was the tosh I was talking? I believed that it was necessary for many plants and insects to have co-evolved, if those insects were to find plants for their larvae to feed on. In other words, it was necessary to grow a larger number of native plants. The evidence is simply not there, according to Thompson; only a comparatively few insects are really picky where they lay their eggs. For a kick-off, our flora (and fauna, come to that) is almost identical, if much poorer, than that of continental Europe, since we were only separated 10,000 years ago, a blink of the eye in evolutionary terms. And it is very similar to the northern temperate flora of the United States, Japan and China, the countries where most of our garden plants originate. So, gardeners have *carte blanche* to grow as many foreign plants as they like.

Thompson would have us alter our mindset, however, if we are better to understand the wildlife in our gardens, and get more fun out of studying it. In other words, we should stop concentrating on a few large animals, such as foxes, which may pass through occasionally, and learn to respect, and foster if we can, the many thousands of creepy-crawly species, on whom all those larger animals depend, and for whom the garden really is home, sweet home.

'Borderlines', *Daily Telegraph*
22 September 2007

I was just going out of the back door the other day, when I was stopped absolutely dead by the presence of a strange (to me) creature on the doormat. It was 3 inches/7 centimetres long, essentially dark brown in colour but with regular horizontal stripes on its back, a small curved horn at one end and, at the other, two baleful dark eyes, which stared at me out of a pale face. I was mystified, as was the spaniel, who sniffed at it disdainfully. This sniffing only seemed to make its dark eyes bulge more prominently.

I cannot deny that I found this small animal momentarily rather alarming.

When I had recovered my poise, having told myself sternly that it was rather smaller than me, I bent down and examined it closely. It was plainly a larva or caterpillar of some sort, but I had no idea what. I went to my natural history reference books for the answer and it didn't take long to discover that it was the larval stage of the elephant hawk moth. On the Internet, I found beautiful photographic images of it. The 'eyes', which had temporarily disconcerted me, were in fact spots, which the animal can enlarge when danger is near. Moreover, it became plain from my researches that all hawk moths have a curved 'horn' on the last segment of their bodies.

I discovered that they were most likely to be seen in August and September, and that the adult moth, which I recalled having seen before in the beam of an outside light, is pink and brown, and quite big for a British moth. I also learned that the larvae's food plants include fuchsias and willowherbs, so I carefully picked up the mat and deposited the creature gently in a flower bed outside, where I knew there was likely to be some *Epilobium montanum*.

In the normal run of things, I find the broad-leaved willowherb a mildly irritating garden weed. It is quite pretty, having small, pink, single flowers and slightly fleshy leaves, and is shorter (at 24 inches/60 centimetres), slighter and much less of a pest than the rosebay willowherb, which everyone knows from the sides of railway tracks or waste ground in late summer. The reason why I weed out *Epilobium montanum* is that it seeds promiscuously and can ruin a colour scheme without even trying. In all the years I have gardened, I have never been able to rid a garden of it. Now, however, I am quite resigned to its presence; indeed, I will take far less care to see that every weed is eradicated on my frequent border rounds.

You probably think it rather strange that I have never seen this 'caterpillar' before, especially since I now remember having seen the adult moth. But our gardens are mysteries to us in many ways, which is one of the most potent reasons why we never tire of spending time in them. Last year, for the first time in my life, I watched, in blank astonishment and admiration, a hummingbird hawk moth hovering over the flowers of *Verbena bonariensis*. This is a migrant from the south of France but, so fast was its wingbeat, and so curved its long proboscis, that even I didn't need to resort to books to discover its identity.

The Spectator
November 2003

I never used to like pampas grass. In fact, I hated it. It was one of the first plants I could name as a child, but not because it appealed to me. There was a large clump in the garden of the school I attended when I was seven and, on almost the first day, I cut my hands painfully and bloodily on its leaves.

If that sounds bizarre, you have never had a close encounter with *Cortaderia selloana*, the imposing, tussock-forming, evergreen pampas grass from temperate parts of South America. 'Cortadera' is a Spanish-American term for 'cutter', so I was not the first person to notice the sharp-toothed margins to the thin, ribbon leaves. The reason I must have been initially attracted to it was the presence of 8-foot/2.5-metre-tall plumes of ivory, silvery-white or pinkish seed heads, which are at their finest at the beginning of the school year in September. These days in gardens it is most often represented by the form 'Sunningdale Silver' or the more compact 'Pumila', and occasionally by two variegated forms, 'Albolineata' and 'Aureolineata'.

Although the grass family generally has become very popular with gardeners in recent years, cortaderia has lost some ground, the victim I think of an association that has built up in the public mind between it and 'suburban' gardens, where it was once a common specimen plant growing in neat lawns. That was never my objection, however, for at a distance it is a stately prospect (and, anyway, what is wrong with the suburban garden?), but I have always found it too large and striking to meld easily in bed or border. And I have never wanted to grow a plant that I, and my inquisitive children, would have to treat with great circumspection.

Although easy enough to grow, pampas grass is a bit of pain when mature, for the inner leaves die yet do not shrivel, so have to be cut and removed. Most people baulk at doing that, unless their hands are clad in leather gauntlets, so the tradition has grown up of setting fire to the old leaves in the autumn or winter. Which is fun, incidentally, although not to be recommended if the clump is close to the house.

My objections to this plant were severely undermined recently, however, after I read an article in *The Field* (the 'hedgerow *Spectator*') about the famous West Barsham wild grey partridge shoot in Norfolk and its legendary keeper, Ted Streeter. A most thoughtful man, plainly, he has taken to planting strips of pampas grass to provide shelter for the English partridge whose welfare and conservation he fosters. The wild grey partridge (as opposed to the red-legged French partridge) is a most particular bird. It is highly territorial, but can be fooled into putting up with smaller territories if it can hear but not see other birds. It likes to be dry and warm (rain cannot easily penetrate a fully grown cortaderia clump), yet able to see out, and needs to be safe from the predatory sparrowhawk. Pampas grass provides winter shelter for insects, and larvae for the chicks in spring. This plant somehow fulfils many of the English partridge's needs, although it takes a near-genius to have made the connection.

Such matters are much in my mind, and possibly in that of my Labrador, Kipling, at the moment. You may think that 1 November is just another autumn Saturday but, to him, it is a red letter day. He has waited nine months, with increasing impatience as the weather has grown colder, for the first day of his pheasant and French partridge picking-up season. He doesn't get many days work but each blissfully punctuates the boredom and pointlessness of a pet's life. And for me, the chance to collaborate so closely with an animal, who does what he does through a happy mix of instinct, breeding and training, means that I now know something of the magic – in miniature, of course – that a huntsman feels when working his pack of hounds.

Today, Kip and I will stand in a wood, many yards behind the 'guns', watching and waiting. I will lean against a tree but he, though given to the Labrador Lean at home, will sit bolt upright, ears and nose twitching compulsively. For this is Business. I will note the colours of the leaves, spiralling downwards in the still air, the clean black ash buds, the progress of a honeysuckle entwined round an oak, the nascent buds of hellebore flowers. We will listen for the blast on the policeman's whistle and gunshots, then count (yes, I mean both of us) and mark the fallers. And when the noise and press and flurry of action is over, I will lean once more on a tree and idly wonder what the field hedges would look like were they topped with waving plumes of pampas grass.

INDEX